Chosen
to Witness His Greatness

JANICE EMAN-HENSHAW

WESTBOW
PRESS®
A DIVISION OF THOMAS NELSON
& ZONDERVAN

WestBow Press books may be ordered through booksellers or by contacting:

WestBow Press
A Division of Thomas Nelson & Zondervan
1663 Liberty Drive
Bloomington, IN 47403
www.westbowpress.com
1 (866) 928-1240

Scripture quotations taken from the Amplified® Bible (AMP),
Copyright © 2015 by The Lockman Foundation Used by permission. www.Lockman.org

Scripture taken from the King James Version of the Bible.

ISBN: 978-1-9736-6927-2 (sc)
ISBN: 978-1-9736-6929-6 (hc)
ISBN: 978-1-9736-6928-9 (e)

Library of Congress Control Number: 2019909919

Print information available on the last page.

WestBow Press rev. date: 8/21/2019

Chosen
to Witness His Greatness

JANICE EMAN-HENSHAW

WESTBOW
PRESS®
A DIVISION OF THOMAS NELSON
& ZONDERVAN

WestBow Press books may be ordered through booksellers or by contacting:

WestBow Press
A Division of Thomas Nelson & Zondervan
1663 Liberty Drive
Bloomington, IN 47403
www.westbowpress.com
1 (866) 928-1240

ISBN: 978-1-9736-6927-2 (sc)
ISBN: 978-1-9736-6929-6 (hc)
ISBN: 978-1-9736-6928-9 (e)

Library of Congress Control Number: 2019909919

Print information available on the last page.

WestBow Press rev. date: 8/21/2019

I dedicate this book to my Lord and Savior Jesus Christ.

I honor my father and mentor, the late Melton Peter Hypolite. He was unique and unarguably authentic in his love for Jesus Christ. Challenged, his earlier years in life were quite frustrating; his latter became glorious when he finally surrendered all to Christ. Daddy was and still is inspirational in my life. I miss him dearly. The declarations he made over me as a child, has been fulfilled through the love I finally came to know in Jesus Christ. I am grateful for Daddy believing in me. Melton Hypolite - September 10, 1951–April 28, 2012

Contents

Acknowledgements

I want to thank my loving, caring, and supportive husband, Francis Eman-Henshaw. He has been highly instrumental in making this book a reality. I could not have done this without him. Francis has unselfishly given me the flexibility of being available to pray and minister to those the Lord has placed in my path from early morning to late evenings. His love for the Lord is expressed through his reverence of the Lord's call over my life and his own. My husband's words of encouragement keep me at peace and focused, knowing that the Lord is working through both of us, orderly. I love you Francis.

I also thank my sweet and endearing grandmother Goldie Mae Robertson. She is one testimony that all things are possible with our Lord. Throughout this book, she has only spoken words of encouragement. Her words of confidence in me echo the words of my late father's. I love you Grand-ma.

I also want to thank my beautiful dear mother, Vivian Mary Trosclair, who has impacted my life throughout the years. The grace of God over her life has given her strength in areas she had not known was possible. She persevered to raise five little ones despite barriers that tried to rob her of her peace and many times even her very life. I thank her for seeing it through. I love you momma.

I say thank you to my exceptional daughter, Britny Michelle Isesele. She has been strategic in the entire book project. Britny has been the spiritual visionary alongside with me during this whole journey. Although she is actively pursuing her degree, married, and care for my four little adorable grandbabies that require her full attention and service, my daughter has played a significant role in capturing the beautiful cover that represented the image the Lord has placed in my heart. I say thank you for reading my drafts and praying with me throughout the process. I say thank you for believing in me and being the light that God has called you to be. There is no other mother-daughter relationship to mimic ours. I am grateful.

I want to thank my son, (by marriage and heart), Travelle Eman-Henshaw, who also played a crucial role in selecting the theme for my book cover. The time and dedication he sacrificed apart from his studies are much appreciated. He has helped me to remain focused on making a vision a reality. I thank him for believing in me.

I want to thank my son Ernest Joseph Hypolite for taking the time to read my drafts and appreciate the importance of spreading the love of Jesus Christ. I thank him for those late-night discussions regarding the passages within the book and providing your honest feedback. I thank him for believing in me.

I want to thank my son, Blaine Anthony Hypolite for his overall support and encouragement to pursue the endeavors that the Lord has placed in my heart. I thank him for his diligence, especially during the marketing phase. I thank him for believing in me.

I want to thank my daughter, (by marriage and heart), Folarin Eman-Henshaw for her overall support and encouragement during the book project. I thank her for extending herself in the backdrop.

I want to thank my dearest sister and closest friend Doctor Faati Isass Myers and her wonderful husband Robert Myers. I thank them for their words of encouragement. Dr. Fati's love and words of wisdom are priceless. Her level of importance goes beyond her profession, but she always makes herself available to me. Her prayers and influence have been impactful during the book project. Her counsel and instructions have taken my health to the level of perfection that the Lord originally intended for me. Every diet regimen she prescribed; I have followed. This has helped me to remain focused and energetic. I am forever grateful.

I want to thank the publishing company, Westbow Press, for its patience and diligence in aiding me during this entire project.

Introduction

The screen door slammed behind me as I rushed into Grandma's shack with a dirty doll in my hand. Gasping for breath, I needed to clarify my actions before my grandmother decided to chase me with her broom. "I found her in the ditch, Grandma. She is the baby doll I have wanted. I only need soap and water."

My grandmother chuckled. She cupped her hands to her mouth and spewed out Creole words I did not recognize. "Lil gal," she retorted while struggling to collect herself. It was random when she used our names. "Take your doll in the bathroom! She smells terrible!" She understood my adamancy about keeping the doll and gave me dishwashing liquid and a bucket of water.

This doll won my affection despite her dirty hair and body. The stench did not affect me. Someone abandoned her, believing she was no longer good enough. My cousins had looked at me with disgust when I lifted her from the ditch. However, the value I placed on her was nonnegotiable and called for no one else's approval.

Her locks were grimy. It required most of my attention. I continued to bathe the rest of her body. I changed her bathwater three times and allowed her to soak for an hour. She looked just as I had imagined. I named her Patricia.

What is the relevance of this story? God showed me a revelation about that day as I meditated one early afternoon. He wants me to Himself. The Lord looks at me with joy, excitement, compassion, and love. He picked me! And I responded. Patricia accepted everything I did to her, not knowing what she did to deserve it. Envision the love that the Lord has for you. Every other opinion is insignificant—even your own.

I still remember how lonely I felt during my childhood years. That void continued into my adult years with the wrong idea of being a "good person." It frustrated me. I had lost my identity. But the Lord opened my eyes. We must discover our identity in Jesus Christ. We try to repair ourselves, but we can't. He chooses us despite our failures. Please be open-minded and patient with me as I expose this truth with supporting scriptures throughout this book.

CHAPTER 1

He Chose to Love You

I had conversations with the Lord at nine years old. I wasn't sure if He heard me or even viewed my concerns as significant. I had learned this practice one day as I witnessed my father looking up to the ceiling with such intensity. His lips were moving, while no sound was coming out. After he had finished, he kissed the cross he was wearing around his neck. Intoxicated, his eyes were in tears as he looked at me and explained that he kissed the cross because, to him, it was a representation of Jesus Christ.

I couldn't understand it, but as I reflect on that day, I believe his expressions resulted from feeling regret and disappointment in himself. Dad had experienced broken promises, feelings of failure, and the desire to get overall approval. He was a confused little boy who grew up not knowing how to trust, while trying to cover shame, guilt, loneliness, abandonment, and not knowing the Lord.

Many of us, like my father, take so much of the hurt we have endured over time, and we misappropriate it into our own method of decision-making. And once we have exhausted our efforts of trying to discover the solution to our anxieties and lack of peace, we eventually look to a higher power, hoping that we can connect with something greater than our limited existence. The Lord has purposely designed human beings to depend on Him.

My father's hurt was so much more than I could grasp because of my ignorance concerning the weight that life and wrong choices could bring. However, despite challenges, God cares about everything concerning us. It may not look like it initially, but the Lord provides the grace needed. He supplies it for the believer and the nonbeliever. The rain falls on the just and the unjust.

Mimicking my father, I would enter the bathroom closet, or my room closet, when my sister wasn't present, and I would talk to God. Most of the time, I was in tears, angered about something. On the good days, I asked the Lord to give my baby doll, Patricia, the ability to talk. I would close my eyes tightly and pray that I would hear a sound from her. It never happened. Later in life, I realized that I had been practicing engaging with God, whom I didn't truly know but had hoped was real. This example is the recipe for having a superficial relationship with the Lord, based on human imaginations. In the beginning stages, it's forgivable, as long as it is short-lived. However, it can be dangerous. The enemy preys on ignorance.

Thankfully, years later I graduated to a better relationship with the Lord, through His written word. However, my greatest struggle was trying to figure things out on my own (self-righteousness). I believed that Jesus died for my sins. However, I could not make the connection of how his death and resurrection affected the way for me to live my life. I didn't understand the importance of knowing and appreciating what the Lord did for me.

Intellectually, I could articulate my faith. But spiritually, I was lacking the ability to surrender everything about myself to trust the Lord Jesus with my thoughts and actions. That deficiency of not knowing how to rely on the Lord was what stalled my ability to progress in a genuine relationship with Him for many years. I had yet to grasp being supernaturally translated out of the realm of death I had unknowingly been born into and planted into the realm of life because I accepted the invitation given me when I sincerely confessed Jesus as my Savior.

> For He has rescued us and has drawn us to Himself from the dominion of darkness, and has transferred us to the kingdom of His beloved Son, in whom we have redemption [because of His sacrifice, resulting in] the forgiveness of our sins [and the cancellation of sins' penalty]. (Colossians 1:13 AMP)

> Jesus Christ, the [g]faithful and trustworthy Witness, the [h]Firstborn of the dead, and the Ruler of the kings of the earth. To Him who [always] loves us and who [has once for all] [i]freed us [or washed us] from our sins by His own blood (His sacrificial death). (Revelations 1:5 AMP)

Just as I knew what I needed to do to make my doll clean without her doing any washing of her own, the Lord made the provisions to make every human being clean by freely giving us His Son as the sacrifice that would wash us in His blood.

A believer only believes because the Holy Spirit of God has revealed Jesus Christ to his spirit. Automatically, this individual becomes a new being and has an unquenchable desire to know more of his Lord and Savior. During this quest, he wants to share his personal experience/ testimony. He is also on the lookout for a mentor, especially if he doesn't belong to a local church. He inventories his friends, old habits, and, in most cases, his ability to change himself. Although it is with good intentions that you want to change yourself, you can't, and that is why you need a savior. Below are a few questions to help you consider whether you are confident in who you are as a born-again Christian. If you have not yet received Jesus as your personal Lord and Savior, allow the Holy Spirit of God to show Him to you plainly and receive Him by faith.

- What would happen to you if you came face-to-face with the creator of the universe who gave everything that has existed its existence?
- Would you be afraid?
- Would you feel confused?
- Would you feel angry with yourself because you would wish you had lived a better life?
- Would you feel ashamed?
- Would you wonder if He would send you into eternal damnation?
- Would you beg His forgiveness for the wrong things you did on earth?

If the answer is yes to any of these questions, I urge you to consider the level of revelation you have in what happened to you when you received Christ as your personal Savior. Meditate on what you have just read, knowing that your Father in heaven loves you. Get a greater revelation of God's love for you through the Holy Spirit. He is the teacher that reveals God's Word, which is His love to your spirit.

> Therefore, there is now no condemnation [no guilty verdict, no punishment] for those who are in Christ Jesus [who believe in Him as personal Lord and Savior]. For the law of the Spirit of life [which is] in Christ Jesus [the law of our new being] has set you free from the law of sin and of death. (Roman 8:1–2 AMP)

Note: The word "revelation" in this context is receiving information that the Holy Spirit of God has shown you. He expands our understanding to a greater level of knowledge based on the holy scriptures. It is an insight into a matter that arouses a conviction within your spirit, causing thoughts to change and action to follow.

SUPERNATURAL ENCOUNTER #1

This leads me to an encounter I'd like to share with you that happened in 1993. My comprehension of the scriptures was limited. I didn't belong to a local church, and I was not active in any fellowship. Sparingly, I would listen to a particular minister on TBN and grasp what I could. Inconsistently, I read and tried to understand the Bible. I wanted to know more about God, and I wanted to go to church, but I just couldn't seem to find one that didn't seem phony or rehearsed. I wanted something real.

One day, around four thirty in the morning, while I was asleep in bed, I experienced my spirit leaving my body. It was so peaceful. I remember feeling lighter than a feather as I swayed in an upward direction. I could even see the beautiful, deep blue skies in the backdrop.

The stars were bright and distinctively noticeable. Suddenly I awoke, and I realized that I would meet Jesus.

I looked down, and I could see my body in a cradle position, still asleep in my bed. I tried to push myself to go back down, but I had no control; I continued to travel up. Desperately, in fear, I pleaded with Jesus to send me back. "I'll be good," I said. "I will live my life only for You. Please send me back." I was so afraid. I was thinking, *What if I dissatisfy God and He sends me to hell?* "Please, Lord, I'll change!" I cried. "I'll live only for You!" I was so panicked. My spirit kept going farther and farther, upward toward Jesus. I didn't see Him, but I knew it inside of me.

Thankfully, I found myself back in my body, back in my bed. I was breathing very hard, as though I had been running. I got out of bed, trying to gather myself after what had just happened. *What happened? How could this be?* I prayed and read my Bible. I searched through the pages, looking for some explanation for what I had just experienced. I didn't have a clue which book in the Bible would help me, but I believed that if the answer was anywhere, it had to be in my Bible. I honestly did not know what to do with myself.

Unsuccessful on my own, at nine o'clock, I headed out the door to find a pastor who would give me some clarity about what had just happened. I knocked on at least five church doors, with no one available. The last facility I visited advised me to attend services the following Sunday, and perhaps I could speak with the pastor then. Well, I attended service, but the pastor was not available to speak with me. It saddened me. I could not get any help. I told God that I would do better. I said I would live for Him. But how?

This is the relevance of my testimony. Because I didn't truly know God, I was afraid of Him. Therefore, I wasn't sure about three things.

1. I didn't know how the Lord felt about me.
2. I didn't know if I was good enough.
3. I didn't know if I would have gone into eternity with Jesus.

In the book of Isaiah, the sixth chapter, Isaiah has an encounter with the Lord. In this vision, He sees the Lord sitting on a throne, with the train of His royal robe filling the temple. He sees seraphim (heavenly beings).

Positioned above the Lord, they are worshipping, saying, "Holy, Holy, Holy is the Lord of Host; the whole earth is filled with His glory." Isaiah is afraid because, at this point, he is reflecting on his sins—much like what I did.

The scripture says that one seraphim takes the burning coal into his hands from the altar and touches Isaiah's mouth. This represented Isaiah's sin being forgiven. Afterward, the Lord sends Isaiah out as His prophet. Isaiah is bold:

> I saw [in a vision] the Lord sitting on a throne, high and exalted, with the train of His royal robe filling the [most holy part of the] temple. Above Him seraphim (heavenly beings) stood; each one had six wings: with two wings he covered his face, with two wings he covered his feet, and with two wings he flew. And one called out to another, saying, "Holy, Holy, Holy is the Lord of hosts; The whole earth is filled with His glory." And the foundations of the thresholds trembled at the voice of him who called out, and the temple was filling with smoke. Then I said, "Woe is me! For I am ruined, Because I am a man of [ceremonially] unclean lips, And I live among a people of unclean lips; For my eyes have seen the King, the Lord of hosts." Then one of the seraphim flew to me with a burning coal in his hand, which he had taken from the altar with tongs. He touched my mouth with it and said, "Listen carefully, this has touched your lips; your wickedness [your sin, your injustice, your wrongdoing] is taken away and your sin atoned for and forgiven." Then I heard the voice of the Lord, saying, "Whom shall I send, and who will go for Us?" Then I said, "Here am I. Send me!" (Isaiah 6 AMP)

Although this scripture references Isaiah's call, it paints a beautiful picture of receiving salvation through the touch of the Holy Spirit. In the beauty of the Lord's presence, your initial response is an authentic evaluation of how unworthy you are. It is at that moment you value the gift of salvation. Perhaps you have confessed Jesus as your Lord by faith, but you have not yet tasted Him. Once you taste Him, you cannot ever denounce Him. I can say this with confidence; it is impossible.

The Holy Spirit draws your entire being to surrender. He makes Jesus real to you. The second you respond, you will possess a deep desire to tell the world of this wonderful testimony. You are now a believer. Isn't this miraculous?

> The Spirit Himself testifies and confirms together with our spirit [assuring us] that we [believers] are children of God. And if [we are His] children, [then we are His] heirs also: heirs of God and fellow heirs with Christ [sharing His spiritual blessing and inheritance], if indeed we share in His suffering so that we may also share in His glory. (Romans 8:16, 17 AMP)

Now, I am certain that this encounter was of God because of the peace and the knowing in my Spirit that it was Jesus. The devil can't give that. The Bible says he is darkness, and there is no light in him at all. That was the day I met my Savior. I knew of the Lord Jesus in my mind, as you will read in chapter 4, but I didn't receive Him in my heart until that day when the Holy Spirit revealed Him. That was when I wanted change. I knew with no doubt that the Lord was a supernatural, supreme being. And today, I testify to anyone who will listen.

Let's recap:

- God brought you into this world because He loves you.
- The Lord wants you to know of His love, so He gave you His Word.
- The Holy Spirit reveals Jesus to you.
- Without God's Word, you will live in constant fear, unsure if you are in good standing with Him.
- He has proven His love by giving you the gift of salvation that is security in Jesus.

Chapter 2

His Ways Are Highest

It's very sad that there are so many believers, even myself earlier in my life, that have their own idea of what God's love should look like. Think about this. Did it look like love when God watched as Jesus was being beaten to an unrecognizable state? Did it look like love when He did nothing as the nails were being hammered into His flesh and through His bones? To the natural man, it's foolish to see love.

However, God's ways are higher than ours. To appreciate such love, the Holy Spirit can only reveal it. To reciprocate such love, it also takes the Holy Spirit to enable you. Jesus believed His Father loved Him and therefore remained faithful and obedient through anything the Father allowed. Our Lord Jesus experienced the full punishment as a human being. He left all of His powers at the throne. The brutality that Jesus suffered was difficult. He was fully man yet fully God.

Have this same attitude in yourselves which was in Christ Jesus [look to Him as your example in selfless humility, who, although He existed in the form and unchanging essence of God [as One with Him, possessing the fullness of all the divine attributes—the entire nature of deity], did not regard equality with God a thing to be grasped or asserted [as if He did not already possess it, or was afraid of losing it]; but emptied Himself [without renouncing or diminishing His deity, but only temporarily giving

> up the outward expression of divine equality and His rightful dignity] by assuming the form of a bond-servant, and being made in the likeness of men [He became completely human but was without sin, being fully God and fully man). (Philippians 2:5–7 AMP)

It was God's love for the world that caused Him to plan everything that Jesus did perfectly, from His entrance into this dark world to His exit. However, it didn't look that way to most. If there were to be a savior of the world, that savior would be wealthy, influential, and a warrior ready to strike down any opposition.

This was what the Hebrew children had in mind for the coming Messiah. They were familiar with the scriptures that spoke of a king that would come from the lineage of King David. That king would restore the kingdom back to them. Below, I summarized the matter.

Let's begin in the Old Testament, when God made a covenant with Abraham.

> Now the Lord said to Abram, "Go from your country and your kindred and your father's house to the land that I will show you. And I will make of you a great nation, and I will bless you and make your name great so that you will be a blessing. I will bless those who bless you, and him who dishonors you I will curse, and in you, all the families of the earth shall be blessed. Abraham had a son named Isaac who had twin boys (Jacob and Esau). Jacob had 12 sons which became the 12 tribes of Israel (a community of people), which were people chosen by God to live according to His ways. These Israelites, (12 tribes), moved to live in Egypt due to a huge famine, and later became slaves. (Genesis 12:1–3 AMP)

God raised the prophet Moses to bring them out of bondage, under the rulership of Pharaoh of Egypt. After much resistance, the Pharaoh allowed the people to go. God instructed Moses to give the people laws to live by.

Later, the children of Israel decided they wanted a king to rule over them like other nations. Although God was not pleased with this, He granted their request, and King Saul, from the small tribe of the Benjamites, became the first appointed by God to rule over their tribes. But Saul didn't obey the instructions that God had given him through the prophet Samuel, so the Lord stripped him of the kingship and chose another king, David, from the tribe of Judah, as his replacement.

After Saul's death, David became king (a man after God's own heart). He united the once-divided tribes and defeated their enemies. During his reign, the land was prosperous and in power.

King David's son, Solomon, became the next king but later worshipped idols. God was not pleased with Solomon. As a result, once-united tribes split. The Israelites continued throughout the Old Testament subjected to oppression from other rulers.

Their hope is in the prophecies that declare the following:

The next King will come from the tribe of Judah.

The next King will be born of a virgin.

The next King will possess the favor of God as King David.

The next King will restore their land back to them so they will live prosperously with the favor of God as their shield.

> For to us, a Child shall be born, to us, a Son shall be given; And the government shall be upon His shoulder, And His name shall be called Wonderful Counselor, Mighty God, Everlasting Father, Prince of Peace. (Isaiah 9:6 AMP)
>
> Therefore the Lord Himself will give you a sign: Listen carefully, the [f]virgin will conceive and give birth to a son, and she will call his name Immanuel (God with us). (Isaiah 7:14 AMP)

Back to my point. God's wisdom surpasses by far human knowledge. Jesus, the Messiah, did not come in the ideal way the children of Israel expected Him to come. The Lord God had hidden it from them. The Messiah's agenda was not only to save the Jewish people, but He came for the nations of the entire world. He didn't come with a physical sword, as the previous kings did by shedding blood, but He came with the spiritual sword, which is the Word of God, to give life, by His choice.

As the Israelites were awaiting their ideal Messiah, He walked, spoke, ate, and drank right in their midst. They didn't recognize Him. They did not trust God who is Jehovah Jireh, their provider. The Lord is wisdom, love, grace, peace, and all that you need Him to be in one. Even though it may not feel like it, He cares for you, and He has made every provision necessary for you to have a glorious life. But you must learn to trust His way.

In reality, the Lord gave His laws only to the Hebrew children. But it was God's abundance of mercy and grace that made us acceptable in His beloved Jesus. Through faith, anyone who confesses from his heart that Jesus as Lord is righteous and therefore saved and included in the promise given to Abraham.

> Through your seed, all the nations of the earth shall be blessed, because you have heard and obeyed My voice. (These are God's words to Abraham. Jesus is the seed of Abraham—according to the flesh.) (Genesis 22:18 AMP)

The promise was spoken to Abraham and his seed. Scripture does not say "seeds," meaning many people, but "seed," meaning one person, who is Christ (Galatians 3:16 AMP).

CHAPTER 3

Get the Vision of Your Newness

I'd like to focus a little more on the concept of the doll being pulled out of the ditch. It's not about the doll, but it shows a wonderful allegory of how we have been pulled out of the darkness and placed in Jesus (light). When I saw the doll, I wanted her. I loved her despite the crusty, dried-up mud she had been sitting in for God only knows how long. And then I washed her.

When God created us, it was His choice. He formed Adam's body from dirt. He gave him spiritual life when He breathed into his nostrils. Sadly, Adam didn't value all that God had blessed him with, and he gave up his rights to Satan, the devil. But God loved us so much that He sent the second and last Adam, Jesus Christ. Our Lord took the authority from the devil and made it available to every human being. We need only to receive it. God no longer sees a believer in the filthy state of sin. Because when you receive Jesus, He washes you in His blood and gives you His righteous identity.

Human nature is constantly seeking further confirmation of what God has already said and even showed. Therefore, it's your job to get the vision of who you are in Christ through the Word of God. You have got to get it into your spirit. Your thoughts will fight you until the day you leave this physical earth. As believers, we depend on the teachings of the Holy Spirit, through scriptures, to catch the vision of who God says we are. When the Lord says He loves you, believe Him. The pettiness of this world cannot compare to the operations of God. As you spend time in His presence, He reveals more and more of Himself to you.

It would be so beneficial for us to be as the doll was in my story, receptive to His grace. See God's strong hand pulling you out of the filth you were born into. See Him putting your sins in Christ at the cross. Now see yourself being buried with Him. Finally, I want you to see your brand-new, ever-so-cleansed spiritual body being resurrected and being placed in Him, at the right hand of your Father. That is where you are today! Glory to our Lord Jesus!

Proclaim that the Lord has translated you into the place of fearlessness. The Word of God associates fear with bondage, but you are free, and God has chosen loved, protected, and blessed you voraciously. The Lord has declared you a son or daughter of the Most High God. You are chosen to be a partaker of God's promise because you believed His testimony of Jesus Christ.

Enjoy your newness in Christ!

Spend time with the Father through the Holy Spirit by doing the following:

- studying the scriptures and meditating on them
- attending church
- fellowship with other believers
- praying in the Holy Ghost on your own
- being conscious throughout the day of the privilege of being a child of God
- singing praises to God in time of worship with a grateful attitude daily

Every day, you will experience a higher level of peace. Now, there will be times when you don't want to do any of these things I mentioned. But I've got good news; this happens to every believer. This is the flesh trying to have its way. Just continue in the direction you are going. The Holy Spirit will strengthen you. In faith, remind yourself that you are making progress because the righteousness of Jesus is the standard placed in you.

So, despite what it may feel like, the truth is what God has already said in His Word. His Spirit will empower you. You cannot live this life in your own strength, child of God. The Lord is your shepherd who causes you to rest in the green pastures of His abundance of grace and wisdom. This is all a part of how you fight the good fight of faith.

Thoughts will try to weigh you down and even try to convince you that you are a phony. Don't fall into that trap. Those thoughts did not come from you. The enemy planted them there. Jesus gave the parable about the weeds that sprung up with the good crop. The farmer did not plant them there; an enemy did it.

> The servants of the owner came to him and said, "Sir, did you not sow good seed in your field? Then how does it have weeds in it?" He replied to them, "An enemy has done this." (Matthew 13:27–28 AMP)

Likewise, as a born-again Christian, you must plant the seed of God's Word in your spirit. The enemy will try to infiltrate your ground, which is your mind, by throwing in filthy thoughts. He may try to remind you of your past mistakes to make you feel guilt and shame. But all those things are old and have passed away. God has given you the mind of Christ. This means that the Holy Spirit will relate the information to you He receives from Jesus. He will remind you of the scriptures you studied concerning a matter.

Another way the enemy tries to confiscate your thoughts is by reeling in old relationships or conversations contrary to the direction that the Lord wants to take you. Those are all weeds springing up in your garden. Use the wisdom that God has given you and pray about those weaknesses. The Lord will strengthen you on the inside. Remember, ignoring those thoughts are not enough. Lift up your hands and thank God that Jesus did it all. Declare unapologetically that you have confidence in what He did. Be consistent. Change will follow.

Manage your daily activities. Choose your conversations wisely. Refuse to compromise because of your surroundings. Christianity is work! The work is establishing principles about yourself that will not lead you to sell out your faith. The Lord will cause you to stand out in the darkness, effortlessly ministering to nonbelievers of the true light.

> And do not be conformed to this world [any longer with its superficial values and customs], but be [c]transformed and progressively changed [as you mature spiritually] by the renewing of your mind [focusing on godly values and ethical attitudes], so that you may prove [for yourselves] what the will of God is, that which is good and acceptable and perfect [in His plan and purpose for you]. (Romans 12:2 AMP)

Be patient with yourself. You need not prove who you are. The Holy Spirit does that as He reveals Christ inside of you. This is how your light shines; you rest. Focus on the wonderful truth that the Lord has placed you on this earth of His own free will. The plans He has for you are good and not evil. You are special in His eyes. He already washed you in the blood of Jesus when you responded to His call. Now He wants to wash your mind daily with His Word so you will function by His Spirit in His divine wisdom.

> So that He, (Jesus), might sanctify the church (believers), having cleansed her by the washing of water with the word [of God]. (Ephesians 5:26 AMP)

CHAPTER 4

Stop Fighting the Water

Let's investigate what it means to allow the Holy Spirit to change you. As a believer, you desire to live your life dedicated to the Lord by projecting it in your daily life. So, perhaps you are even doing some things I've just mentioned, but you continue to struggle. I will share a wonderful revelation of how to stop struggling—how to stop panicking in the water.

At the young and inexperienced age of fourteen, I went to our community park swimming pool with a few of my girlfriends. I didn't intend to swim; I was only planning on getting my legs wet. So, there I was sitting on the edge of the slab, with my eyes closed ever so gently, allowing my legs to get wet. I heard the familiar voices of my friends, their giggling and playful screams, and the splashing of water as usual in the backdrop.

Relaxed, I enjoyed the cool water that sent the sensations of its temperature to the rest of my body. Then, suddenly, one of my friends pushed me in the water! I panicked while moving my arms and legs out of control in the water. I tried so hard not to swallow the water, but I had to cry out for help. I heard shouting, someone saying, "Just stand up, Janice! Just stand up!" In the commotion's midst, I could make out one of my friends laughing as another friend came and lifted my body to a standing position. I was furious. Everyone was having a wonderful time at my expense. And finally, I realized that the water was less than four feet deep.

In the scenario above, the water is a representation of the Holy Spirit. The act of me being pushed into the water was an example of unexpected challenges presenting themselves in our lives. Our reaction to those unexpected events will depend solely on whether we are prepared spiritually and physically. Life happens. God's standard is our best life. Trusting Him is a purposeful act. The Holy Spirit wants to play His part, but we have to allow Him.

As we mature, we learn to trust and rely more on the Father and less on ourselves. I panicked in the water because I was afraid of drowning. It is not an uncommon thing for anyone who does not know how to swim to feel afraid if thrown into the water. But as I tried to keep myself afloat, I only made unnecessary movements that didn't even help my situation. I was fighting the water.

In the scriptures, the disciples looked in awe as they witnessed Jesus walking on water. Inspired by what he saw, Peter asked Jesus to give him the ability to walk on water. Jesus granted his request, and Peter walked on the water just as Jesus did. However, when the storms, waves, and winds became ferocious, Peter panicked and drowned. Jesus lifted him up from drowning, and they both walked back to the boat.

> And in the fourth watch of the night (3:00–6:00 a.m.) Jesus came to them, walking on the sea. When the disciples saw Him walking on the sea, they were terrified, and said, "It is a ghost!" And they cried out in fear. But immediately He spoke to them, saying, "Take courage, it is I! Do not be afraid!" Peter replied to Him, "Lord, if it is [really] You, command me to come to You on the water." He said, "Come!" So Peter got out of the boat, and walked on the water and came toward Jesus. But when he saw [the effects of] the wind, he was frightened, and he began to sink, and he cried out, "Lord, save me!" Immediately Jesus extended His hand and caught him, saying to him, "O you of little faith, why did you [c]doubt?" And when they got into the boat, the wind ceased. Then those in the boat worshiped Him [with awe-inspired reverence], saying, "Truly You are the Son of God!" (Matthew 14:22–33 AMP)

After reading the scripture, you could wonder, *Why did Peter doubt?* However, this is what many of us do amid challenges; we panic and ignore the Helper as we try to figure out the answers on our own. However, we need the Holy Spirit. Jesus said that He would ask the Father to send the Holy Spirit to help those who believe in Him. The Holy Spirit has a ministry to give you inside information from the Master. So, in order for the Holy Spirit to aid you, you will need to adjust how you respond in those challenging moments.

Last, acknowledge even the small wins. The Lord loves when we are thankful with the attitude of knowing that whatever He has accomplished for us, His grace did it. When you notice even the slightest behavioral changes in yourself, give Him glory. Celebrate from your spirit and not from your mind. Celebrate in song and dance as you center your thoughts on the redemptive savior, Jesus Christ. Practice thanking Him because you are seeing how much you value Him.

Here are a few confessions to use on your journey:

- Jesus is my Lord; therefore, I am the righteousness of God.
- I am a member of the household of God and a joint heir with Christ.
- I have the Holy Spirit of God living inside of me.
- I am led by the Spirit of God.
- I am a new creation; my past is gone, dead, and buried.
- All things are working together for my good, and I have the mind of Christ. As He is, so am I in this world.
- The powerful Word of God is transforming me from the inside out.
- The powerful Word of God is as a lamp under my feet and a light directing my path.
- I refuse to fear. I refuse to be anxious.
- I have love, patience, temperance, faith, joy, peace, goodness, kindness, and gentleness.
- I am progressing every day.
- I am as a tree planted by the rivers of water and consumed with the anointing of God's presence.

I assume you've gained a better discerning of the blessings you have because you are chosen. And because you are born again, you belong to the family of faith. Your Father in heaven has planted His Spirit inside of you, and He has equipped you with the powerful name of Jesus. Nevertheless, there is so much that I would like to share that I hope will help position you on how to operate in your newly created life. I'd like to use the scripture taken from John, chapter 3, verses 2–21 as a focal point of reference. It's the discussion that occurs between Nicodemus (a ruler of the Jews) and Jesus. I want to show you the insignificant mind-set of an individual who tries to interpret God's Word without being born again.

> Now there was a certain man among the Pharisees named Nicodemus, a ruler (a member of the Sanhedrin) among the Jews, 2 who came to Jesus at night and said to Him, "Rabbi (Teacher), we know [without any doubt] that You have come from God as a teacher; for no one can do these signs [these wonders, these attesting miracles] that You do unless God is with him." (John 3:1–2 AMP)

Nicodemus approached Jesus in the evening. He acknowledged that Jesus was a teacher sent from God. He confessed that he knew that the only way a man could perform miracles was if God was with him. Jesus marveled him. Here is Jesus's reply.

"Verily, verily, I say unto you, except if a man is born again, he cannot see the kingdom of God." (John 3:3 AMP)

Did you catch that? Jesus, in His infinite wisdom, is saying to Nicodemus that the only way he can see (understand) is to be born again (born of the Spirit of God). Note how Nicodemus makes a statement concerning the miracles he witnesses Jesus performing and the response that Jesus gives. Perplexed, Nicodemus questioned the validity of Jesus. Why would God use Jesus? He was only a mere son of a carpenter, as opposed to the "much-esteemed" Pharisees and members of the Sanhedrin.

> Nicodemus said to Jesus, how can a man be born when he is old? Can he enter the second time into his mother's womb and be born? (John 3:4 AMP)

Most likely, you would agree that it was not unreasonable for Nicodemus to ask such a question. To be born again means starting from the beginning. However, this is not a physical womb; it is spiritual.

> Yet to all who did receive Jesus, to those who believed in His name, he gave the right to become children of God - children not born of natural descent, nor of human decision, or a husband's will, but born of God. (John 1:12–13 AMP)

Nicodemus probably scratched his head trying to understand the concepts that Jesus spoke. Most likely, he relied on his human wisdom to help him to understand. But Jesus was no common man speaking ordinary words. He was the Son of God speaking the truth that only a sincere heart would accept.

What's my point? I am stressing the importance of the order of renewing your mind to a state that can grab the whole of spiritual realities. The prerequisite to this is salvation. Anyone can read the Bible. They can get information from within it. However, if the Holy Spirit is not inside of that individual as the official translator, that person will relate from a Nicodemus point of view; his understanding will be unfruitful.

There will be questions that will present themselves in your thoughts. Sometimes, it will be God probing you to help you consider or ponder His Word so you can gain a greater insight. And in other cases, it can be the enemy bringing an accusation against God's Word. He wants to stir up confusion as he did with Adam and Eve in the garden. How can you distinguish? The answer is just below.

> Study and do your best to present yourself approved to God, a workman (tested by trial) who has no reason to be ashamed, accurately handling and skillfully teaching the word of truth. But avoid irreverent babble and godless chatter (with its profane, empty words), for it will lead to further ungodliness. (2 Timothy 2:15–16 AMP)

Curiosity invited Nicodemus to meet with Jesus that night. It's conceivable he was fulfilling his role as a Jewish leader to scope out Jesus's claims. However, the book of John also gives an account that Nicodemus appeared at the burial of Christ. He further assisted Joseph Arimathea (a disciple of Jesus) in preparing Jesus's body. He even purchased expensive spices to assist in the burial. His actions were significant. The Bible doesn't indicate whether Nicodemus converted, but I think his actions spoke volumes.

Again, it is important to understand God's Word in the right context. As you become more acquainted with the scriptures, the Holy Spirit will explain things to you. He will reveal to your heart truth or error regarding the things you hear and see. But you must trust that God's Word is final by faith.

Nicodemus recalled the scriptures that spoke of the evidence of the coming Messiah. He couldn't deny that Jesus meant the qualifications of those prophecies. However, it was still necessary for him to proclaim the Lordship of Jesus Christ by faith before the Lord would remove the blindfold. Remember, the Holy Spirit reveals Jesus to a nonbeliever before He receives Him, but the nonbeliever must receive by faith.

A believer has a responsibility to discover who he/she is in Christ by studying the scriptures. Salvation is the beginning stages of Christianity. Just like in the natural, you supply your spirit the nutrients to grow into maturity. A believer gets those nutrients in the Holy Scriptures captured in the Bible. And the Bible is all about Jesus and the Father's everlasting love for you. He wants a genuine relationship with us. Not a religious, superficial one with a human being's assumptions but instead based on His Word.

To be effective in studying God's Word, get connected to a ministry that teaches the grace of God through the redemptive blood of Christ and His righteousness.

SUPERNATURAL ENCOUNTER #2

I'd like to share this encounter I had with the Lord that opened my eyes to His love for me despite myself. It happened one day as I was visiting a local church around 2002. A friend of mine from high school had invited me to attend. A customer from her place of employment had previously invited her. By this time, I was attending church regularly and sincerely spending time with the Lord. However, my friend had not been going to church, so I accompanied her since she had grown cold to the things of God.

At the beginning of the service, the minister instructed everyone to pray in tongues. I was so excited because I had just recently prayed in tongues only two months ago. I guess I felt a sense of maturity. The pastor spoke to one of her members in front of me and said, "Pray with this sister over here." My friend was standing right next to me. I thought, *she's the one who needs someone to pray with her, not me. But, oh well, I guess I'll bless this sister.* As the lady prayed with me, a powerful force came all over me. The pastor said, "Bring her here." I remember someone helped me to the front of the church. There was such a strong energy of God's presence over me; I had no strength.

As I went to the front, a covering swept over me as though it encapsulated me in a wave of water without the wetness. The warmth of His being overshadowed me as He gently pressed me to the floor. I was so close to the Master. I could not imagine this place outside of this universe. It had no sound yet a loud silence of serenity. The communication of love was beyond words. God is real. His love is real. I have no explanation for why this extraordinary experience happened, but it did. And I'm grateful. I experienced so much joy, so much peace, so much love! He chose to do it. I earned none of it.

I will never forget the expression on my friend's face when I finally picked myself off the floor. I didn't hear one word of the sermon. As I made my way to the pew, tears were still actively flowing down my face. My friend asked me if I was okay. She looked so confused. She did not realize they were tears of joy. Like Nicodemus, she could not relate to the place I found myself. There were no words to express the love that was overwhelmingly over my entire being.

Brothers and sisters, don't understand God through the imaginations of human intellect that may have built up inside you through religious attitudes, worldly movies, music, and conversations. They are useless. Instead, patiently allow the Holy Spirit to open your mind to His thoughts through His Word. You will learn of the Father's great love for you. Nothing else matters in the presence of God. He lives inside of every one of His children. And He wants to reveal more of Himself to you. He wants this for all of us. You can't strive for this love. He expects you to take it into your being,

> Come close to God [with a contrite heart] and He will come close to you. (James 4:8 AMP)

I know that God was lavishing me with His love. It was a divine appointment the Lord had for me. I was truly seeking Him in that period of my life. I was so hungry for the Lord. Receive the love He has for you in its fullness by embracing it. Experience His presence personally by allowing yourself to trust Him. Enforce the truth in your thoughts. He willingly brought you into this world for good and not bad.

I would love to testify that at that point I learned that it was the Holy Spirit that would perfect everything about me and that I flowed in the wonderful grace of God. I wanted to, but I didn't know how. I had yet to understand the authority and grace God had given me in Christ. I figured the Lord only reserved those things for pastors. Unfortunately, I continued on an unpleasant journey of trying to earn God's love (self-righteousness). To help us understand this mind-set, let's analyze Nicodemus and the queries he expresses to Jesus.

> (Jesus says to him), "That which is born of the flesh is flesh (the physical), and that which is born of Spirit

> (Spirit of God), is a spirit. Do not be surprised that I have told you that you must be born again (spiritually transformed, renewed, and sanctified). The wind blows where it wishes and you hear its sound, but you do not know where it is coming from and where it is going; so it is with everyone who is born of the Spirit. (John chapter 3:6–8 AMP)

Jesus spoke powerful words to a man who could only relate to things of the flesh (physical) realm. In the following verse, Nicodemus responds by saying, "How can these things be?" (ninth verse). If you recall in my testimony from chapter 1, as I awoke from my encounter with the Lord, that was the question that sparked from my thoughts. *How could this be? How is it possible for a person to separate from its body and return—and witness it?* That's what happens to a mind ignorant of the spirit realm.

Again, the Holy Spirit is your teacher. He helps you to renew your mind. Simultaneously, He needs you to input the written word of God into your mind. And even after that, it's crucial for you to develop times of meditation to get it in sync with your new spirit. Nicodemus was familiar with the scriptures written from the days of old, but he lacked the interpretation only God could release. Jesus spoke words to Nicodemus, but he only heard them in parables. The encounter I experienced when the Lord poured Himself all over me is not significant to someone whom he has not revealed Himself to. However, the ones who know Him rejoice all together in knowledge.

Let's continue with the following scriptures:

> "Jesus answered and said, you are Israel's teacher and you do not understand these things? Very truly I tell you, we speak of what we know, and we testify to what we have seen, but still you people do not accept our testimony. I have spoken to you of earthly things and you do not believe; how then will you believe if I speak of heavenly things? No one has ever gone into heaven except the

> one who came from heaven—the Son of Man." (John 3:10–13 AMP)

Wow! Jesus is not apologetic about speaking truth. His boldness is incomparable as He addresses him with such audacity. He said "we" speak of what "we" know and testify. Who is He referring to when He says "we"? He's speaking about Himself and the prophets that came before Him. They (the Old Testament prophets and John the Baptist) all testified of His coming, but the Pharisees, Sanhedrin, and many other Jews didn't believe. Jesus is proclaiming that not only is He a Prophet, but He is "the Greatest Prophet," also the Chosen One, the Anointed One, the one who came from heaven, God in the flesh. The one about whom John the Baptist said, "The One that comes after me is preferred before me."

Jesus told Nicodemus that He and the other prophets spoke of what they had seen. God revealed Himself plainly to the prophets, but the Israelites refused to believe the truth. When the Lord reveals Himself to you, be careful not to miss the opportunity to receive His testimony.

> Jesus said to him (his disciple), "Have I been with you for so long a time and you do not know Me yet, Philip, nor recognize clearly who I am? Anyone who has seen Me has seen the Father. (John 14:9)

Let's recap this chapter a so we stay on point:

- You have been born of the Spirit of God.
- You study God's Word, so you know the truth.
- As you study God's Word, the Holy Spirit helps you to interpret it rightly.
- God loves you and has chosen to establish you for success through His Word.

Excellent! Let's continue.

CHAPTER 5

Learn to Trust Him

We have revealed powerful foundations to gain better insight into what it means to be chosen by God. Now, let's dive even deeper concerning God's love for you. This love is not only for the believer, but it's also for the nonbeliever. God has chosen to love you and me despite ourselves. Thank God! I urge you to make the greatest attempt to receive this next statement very well. Let it continue to marinate in your mind until it finally sinks down in your spirit. It's God's nature to love. Aren't we blessed? More than we can imagine.

Remember, in the first chapter, I said, "As human beings, we can never truly comprehend the love that God has for us." The wisdom of God's Word that says He uses the foolish things of this world to confound the wise. I want you to see His love through the wise and purposeful words that Jesus says to Nicodemus. The Lord Jesus is using Old Testament scriptures to show Nicodemus God's hidden plan of salvation through Him (Jesus).

> As Moses lifted up the serpent in the wilderness, even so, must the Son of man be lifted up: that whosoever believe in Him should not perish, but have eternal life. For God so loved the world, that He gave His only begotten Son, that whosoever believe in Him should not perish but have everlasting life. (John 3:14–16 AMP)

This is truly the wisdom of God! Don't grow frustrated if you are not clear on what the fourteenth verse is saying. Let's shed some light on it. These are only a few highlights.

Who was Moses?

- He was a Hebrew born as a slave and a prophet of God.
- He was adopted as the son of the Pharaoh's daughter, in Egypt, where he lived for forty years.
- He was chosen to lead the children of Israel out of Egypt (a place they had been in bondage).
- He split the Red Sea, by the power of God, as a way of escape for the Hebrews.
- God gave him the laws (commandments) to govern the Israelites.
- He was overall respected by the Hebrew people.

Once you study the first five books of the Bible, you will have more clarity.

Let's continue.

Even though God used Moses and performed many miracles while leading the Israelites out of Egypt, the Hebrew children still did not learn to trust God. They murmured and complained against God because they were angry. They disapproved of the "unfavorable" conditions on their journey to the Promised Land. Although they were in the wilderness, God provided them manna (a light form of bread) and water daily, but still, it wasn't enough. In His anger toward their behavior, God caused serpents to bite the Israelites. Thousands died. The Lord made a way of escape for His people. (Please note, this is one of many incidents that happened under the old covenant of the law. Under that covenant, God punished disobedience.)

Jesus is revealing God's wisdom by prophesying to Nicodemus, reminding him of the time of judgment against the Israelites, when the Lord used the unlikely form of the bronze serpent to heal the Hebrews of their sin. The Father's Son will step into time through the vehicle of a virgin woman. He will be innocent of all charges. Willingly, He will take the sins of the entire human race on Himself and allow Himself to be put to death. The Lord God will receive His Son's innocent blood as a sacrifice for the sins of the world and finally judge and declare Him righteous. The Lord will then resurrect Him in bodily form. And He will heal all who will look upon Him and repentantly declare Him Lord. This is the reality for the Hebrew tribes and everyone who believes.

Jesus's sacrifice at the cross was God's mercy toward humans who are ignorant of their corrupt nature.

> For the message of the cross is foolishness [absurd and illogical] to those who are perishing and spiritually dead [because they reject it], but to us who are being saved [by God's grace], it is [the manifestation of] the power of God. (1 Corinthians 1:18 AMP)

CHAPTER 6

Yield to God's Thoughts

God has given us His Word so He may impart spiritual understanding to our minds. As we are renewing our minds, we can communicate effectively and confidently with our Father. A renewed mind causes a believer to know God's love for him. Overtime, your language changes, your attitude changes, your opinions change, and they become whatever God says. Your faith increases, and joy explodes from the inside of you because the Word of God has shown you wonderful things, such as the truth that you are only temporarily on this earth, and during your stay, you have a purpose much bigger than your own personal wants. We serve a big and powerful God in every sense of the word. Yet, while we are growing, he meets us at our level.

> Therefore, I urge you, brothers and sisters, by the mercies of God, to present your bodies [dedicating all of yourselves, set apart] as a living sacrifice, holy and well-pleasing to God, which is your rational (logical, intelligent) act of worship. And do not be conformed to this world [any longer with its superficial values and customs], but be [c]transformed and progressively changed [as you mature spiritually] by the renewing of your mind [focusing on godly values and ethical attitudes], so that you may prove [for yourselves] what the will of God is, that which is good and acceptable

> and perfect [in His plan and purpose for you]. (Roman
> 12:1–2 AMP)

In the book of Genesis, the Lord announced the first record of history. He created time for man. As we mature spiritually, God allows our perception to broaden, therefore bringing us into an even closer insight of who He is through His Word. The Lord God placed Adam and Eve in the position of rest. They could fellowship with the Lord and enjoy the beauty of His creation.

Recall that after the devil deceived them, God had them cast out of the garden, which was away from His presence. They were no longer in fellowship with God. Adam handed his God-given authority to the enemy and became spiritually dead and powerless. His wife and any future human beings were all born into that same fate. So that includes us.

You may wonder, How is that love? Why didn't God shield them from the devil's tactics? Actually, He did. God gave Adam and Eve the only needed weapon in the garden, truth. However, God gave them free will. They could have chosen rightly! They were free to appreciate the goodness of God. Free to eat all they wanted to enjoy, with only one exception: do not eat of the tree of the knowledge of good and evil.

I remember when I was about twelve years old how angry I felt toward Adam and Eve for disobeying God by eating that fruit. But as I matured in life through my studies of God's Word and reflecting on the choices I've made, I no longer criticized and placed blame on them. Instead, I trust God's Word that says I should not place any confidence in my ability (the flesh). I must always pray and ask Him first and then act accordingly. We must allow the Lord God to train us in His Word. Believe that our limited view will lead us down the wrong path. Since He created every path, He knows its destination.

This is the love of God. He is the life giver. He loves you so much that He gave you the truth, which is His Word. Remember, He told Adam, "The day you eat of the forbidden fruit, you will surely die." Adam chose death over life. But what caused Adam to heed the voice of the serpent whom he did not know over the voice of God, who gave him life? It was his ability to question any situation. The Lord does not want us to live in ignorance. He blessed us with brains that gather intelligence. But that information is not always accurate. Adam put his faith in a created being as opposed to the Creator of all things.

When the serpent presented his lies, Adam's position was to stand firm on the foundation of the Supreme being who gave him dominion over the fish of the sea, the birds of the air, and every living thing that moved on the earth (Genesis 1:28). However, he allowed the enemy to deceive him, whom he had authority over.

Why would God create Adam only to give him a miserable life? It was always His plan to give Adam the good things. But the Lord also wanted a relationship with him—a relationship built on trust. The Lord engineered him that way. He created Eve because He knew of the necessity of companionship. However, wicked actions will taint the relationship, and it cannot continue.

One morning as I was meditating in God's presence, He unfolded mysteries concerning this. This revelation blew me away. He showed me a revelation of Jesus and His church and the marriage that exists between a man and a woman. The Lord said that He purposely designed it so that a man should only enter a woman with her consent. She can either receive him or reject him. If she rejects him, and he forces himself in her, the law considers it rape; this is a violation. If she receives him, the Lord consider the two legally one.

God will not violate His own laws He has established. He will not force Himself on anyone. Once rejected, He will not enter. The Lord God wants to have an intimate relationship that has nothing to do with anything physical. He wants us to experience the pleasures of His presence living inside of a believer. Whenever you receive Jesus as your Lord and Savior, He comes to live inside of you. Your body belongs to Him. Jesus is the vine, and you are the branches. The offspring of that relationship is the fruit of the spirit.

> But the fruit of the Spirit [the result of His presence within us] is love [unselfish concern for others], joy, [inner] peace, patience [not the ability to wait, but how we act while waiting], kindness, goodness, faithfulness,

> gentleness and self-control. Against such things there is
> no law. (Galatians 5:22, 23 AMP)

As children of God, the following applies:

- We are alive, and God has translated us out of the kingdom of darkness, which is deception, and into the kingdom of light, which is truth.
- The Holy Spirit comes to live in us.
- We live in the realm of love.
- We are clothed with the glory of our Lord, and He declares us righteous.
- We dwell in the secret place of the Most High, who has made us partakers of His divine nature.
- We have a right to call on Abba (Daddy) Father because of Jesus.

Connect to see the spiritual transaction that took place when Jesus came down on this earth. He allowed Himself to suffer and die on the cross, innocent before God. Jehovah God raised Him from the dead and declared Him righteous. Finally, He conquered spiritual death for all humanity. Jesus took the authority that Satan stole and gave it back to every believer. This is the supernatural advantage that can never be reversed.

Our God is merciful, and He always creates a way of escape. He mapped out everything long before He put anything into existence. Adam didn't realize how big his Maker was, at least not at first. But truly he's no exception. It takes consistent quality companionship to know the Lord by faith. You can't see Him, so your thoughts will challenge you. And again, you will need the Helper, the Holy Spirit, to press you closer and closer to Jesus.

This is an opportunity to talk about Thomas. He was one of Jesus's disciples but doubted His resurrection. He was with the Christ when He performed many miracles, including raising the dead, opening blind eyes, and healing the sick, and he was also privileged to hear firsthand teachings from the Master. Yet it wasn't enough. It was not until he got physical proof that he finally believed. Our Lord responded by saying, "Blessed are those who believe without seeing."

The significance of being a child of God is the witness of the Holy Spirit. This kind of knowing comes from within your spirit. Thomas was aware that Jesus was the Anointed One because he had witnessed the miracles that justified the Master as the Christ. However, Thomas lacked the confidence to remain rooted in the truth. He was at war with his thoughts.

Believe it or not, many of us, as Thomas, battle with accepting what is the simple truth. Thomas had already figured out why Jesus, the Christ, had come on this earth and exactly what purpose God had given Him; at least in his mind, he did. Like many Jewish people, Thomas wanted a king that would physically defend the children of Israel with the sword, just as the previous ones did. But Jesus was above the other kings and any other that would follow.

Thomas couldn't see that this King fought with a spiritual sword. This King controlled the waters and the winds, and demons were afraid of Him.

But how quickly he forgot. It's because he was so consumed with his way of doing things; he became his own leader. Blinded in his selfish agenda, he missed the wonderful truth that Jesus didn't come for the salvation of only the Jews, but he came for the entire world. Our Lord Jesus had already revealed to His disciples before they put him to death that He was God in the flesh. As simple as it is to embrace this love, we make it difficult through our own reasoning.

Jehovah God created every being without counsel from any man or angel—no one! God is God! Read these wondrous, powerful words the Lord spoke to Job of His Supreme Being:

Then the Lord answered Job out of the whirlwind and said, "Who is this that darkens counsel [questioning my authority and wisdom] By words without knowledge? Now [a]gird up your loins like a man, And I will ask you, and you instruct Me! Where were you when I laid the foundation of the earth? Tell Me, if you know and have understanding. Who determined the measurements [of the earth], if you know? Or who stretched the [measuring] line on it? On what were its foundations fastened? Or who laid its cornerstone … (Job 38 AMP)

Do you know the time when the wild goats of the rock give birth [to their young]? Do you observe the calving of the deer? Can you count the months that they [a]carry offspring, Or do you know the time when they give birth? They kneel down, they bring forth their young, They cast out their labor pains. Their young ones become strong, they grow up in the open field; They leave and do not return to them. Who sent out the wild donkey free [from dependence on man]? And who has loosed the bonds of the wild donkey [to survive in the wild] ... The [flightless] wings of the ostrich wave joyously; With the pinion (shackles, fetters) and plumage of love, For she leaves her eggs on the ground And warms them in the dust, Forgetting that a foot may crush them, Or that the wild beast may trample them. She treats her young cruelly, as if they were not hers; Though her labor is in vain because she is unconcerned [for the safety of her brood], For God has made her forget wisdom, And has not given her a share of understanding. Yet when she lifts herself [b]on high, [So swift is she that] she laughs at the horse and his rider. (Job 39)

Isn't that powerful? I challenge you to read both chapters thoroughly.

The ground did not argue when Jehovah separated the waters to cause a division between sky and land. Nor did the animals that God created without wings put up a debate for the right fly to survive on the land. Instead, they functioned according to an internal instinct of how to live on this land. The Lord God placed everything in them according to His purpose. Did you note some complexities involved as the Lord said that He deprived the ostrich of understanding and that she lacked the wisdom to realize that some things she worked to do to protect her young were useless because she didn't hide them from their predators, nor did she consider her own ignorance of potentially crushing them? She has great wings but can't fly. However, she runs faster than a horse.

It is God who reveals wisdom to the born-again spirit of a man.

Otherwise, our understanding is as futile as the ignorance of the ostrich. Have you ever had a dream and tried to interpret it without the Holy Spirit? You rack your brain trying to piece together the bits and pieces that seem to be out of order. You try to relate the things you saw in the spirit to the things you appear to know of in the physical. Your interpretation will be in error. It's only God's wisdom that will show it to you. This is what He's explaining to Job in the scriptures above.

God is wisdom. It is only at the advantage of the believer to place our trust in the truth. He knows the whole story because He is the author. The Lord gives every man the opportunity to receive the gift of eternal life. That life begins to open our eyes to see as God sees. It's piloted by faith in His Word through the ministry of the Holy Spirit.

See the benefits of salvation that Christ has purchased for you. Other avenues that appear to be the way will misguide you, as they did Adam. Be patient. Sit in God's presence and get to know Him personally. He will take control of your thoughts and cause you to consider the things He has said.

Be consistent in your daily prayer time and don't make it a religious duty. Determine within yourself that you serve a living God who hears you at all times. Speak from your heart. Close your eyes and shut everyone and everything out. Don't look at yourself; see Him. Enjoy His beauty and be grateful for the blood of Jesus. Focus on what Jesus did at the cross. It is His blood that caused you to be exempt from eternal damnation. His blood paid for your weakness and has made you strong in Him. Jesus Christ has made you righteous before God. Reflect about these things in the presence of God. Look away from yourself and just exercise enjoying his presence. God has designed you for greatness, and He wishes for you to prosper in everything you set your heart to do. He's in love with you!

Let's explore more examples of learning how to trust what He says and the struggles of belief. The angel Gabriel appeared before Zacharias, the father of John the Baptist. Gabriel told Zacharias that he would be the father of a son who would be filled with the Holy Spirit at birth and that he would be great in the sight of God. Gabriel appeared to Zacharias because of the prayers he had requested before God. However, Zacharias did not believe God's messenger.

The angel Gabriel exposed God's purpose and plans for Zacharias's son. However, Zacharias wanted an even greater sign to prove that these things were true. What more of a sign could he have wanted than a high-ranking angel, who stands in the presence of God, to give him such a message! But because of his unbelief, the Lord made him dumb (unable to speak) until the appointed time of his son's birth.

Consider this for a minute. Why is it we are constantly looking for more evidence? We mimic the actions of Adam and Eve. We complicate things. God wants us to be as little children, innocent and trusting. As a child of God, He establishes us in His righteousness, by His Word. We exercise our faith in a good God who has purposed us for greatness all to His glory.

I am not insinuating that a believer is someone who never considers a word spoken. The Word of God speaks against ignorance and greatly for knowledge, understanding, and revelation. Scripture tell us to test the spirits to know if they are from God. However, once the Lord has revealed it to our spirits, we need to protect the truth by declaring continually what He has revealed until it comes to pass.

Zacharias was a Levitical priest familiar with the Hebrew scriptures that prophesied of the coming Messiah and the prophet that would come beforehand to call the Jewish people to repentance. He was also familiar with the scriptures that spoke of the angel Gabriel coming to the aid of Daniel during his time of fasting. Yet he could not discern rightly.

The wisdom of this world is no comparison to the wisdom of God. Our minds are finite, no matter how much literature we read. We answer to an infinite God who reveals what He chooses, to whom He chooses, and when He chooses. Salvation is not only for going to heaven, but it's also about living your life on this physical earth according to the household of faith. God has given us the Holy Scriptures as a guide for our walk. As we study the truth, we grow in our faith and expand in His wisdom. We develop a greater level of confidence in the Lord.

However, if we go through the motions by playing church and attending religious ceremonies, then we make the Word of God ineffective in our lives, and we have yet to know Jesus personally. Our Lord says that anyone that comes to Him must come knowing He is a rewarder because you have diligently sought Him through His Word by the spirit. This means your heart must be actively taking part. It's not the action of what you are doing; it is the motive behind the action. It interests God to know you believe Him. He alone is God, and He does what he says. No matter how long it takes. And if it doesn't happen, you continue in patience trusting Him anyway.

After His resurrection, the Lord Jesus walked this physical earth for forty days in His resurrected physical body, openly, so that many could witness. The Lord had prophesied before his death that the people would put him to death. He explained that the Father would resurrect Him. Jesus assured the disciples He would send the Holy Spirit as a comforter and a witness.

The Lord God sent Jesus on earth to complete the purpose of reconciling sinful man back to God. That same Spirit that caused Jesus to open blind eyes, walk on water, heal the sick, and cast out demons is what every believer receives when he confesses Jesus as his personal savior with a believing heart.

So, what is the difference between you and Thomas, or you and Zacharias? Thomas walked with the Christ as proclaimed in the Gospels, and Zacharias received a personal message from God from the high-ranking angel Gabriel. However, they both wanted more proof. You have the Spirit of God living inside of you with an assurance you will spend eternity with Jesus. Do you need more proof?

The Word of God says He is unchanging, and He has given you every spiritual blessing, which by His grace entitles you to live life consistently at the place of rest. Can you see? Why can't we just enjoy God and appreciate the sacrifice He made for us? Put off the old man and wear your new, recreated spirit man! The old man is filled with anger, envy, bitterness, self-destruction, greed, vengeance, pride, loneliness, and cruelty. You have been crucified with Christ. Remember that. You have the right to enjoy your freedom. You are no longer entangled with darkness. You are a believer as long as you confessed Jesus as Lord and Savior over your life from your heart, so enjoy it. Pursue Him with zeal by studying His being, which He has made available through scriptures.

CHAPTER 7

Humility Is Key

I'm sure you, like everyone else in this world, have had an overflow of unacceptable behaviors that have latched on over the years for as long as you can remember. It's okay. Because no matter how horrible your past may seem, the blood of Jesus gave you a fresh start when you turned your heart over to Him. He made everything about your life stain-free! If you have ever watched some of the detergent commercials, each claims to have a stronger stain-fighting power than the other.

However, no matter how much effort the detergent uses to bring the garment to its original state, it can never take away 100 percent of the stain. In fact, the cloth loses its beauty throughout time as it is being washed. Unlike the blood of the Lamb that cleanses us, freeing us from any form of blemish (sin). And the more we realize that truth in our hearts, the more radiant we become.

> And from Jesus Christ, the [g]faithful and trustworthy Witness, the Firstborn of the dead, and the Ruler of the kings of the earth. To Him who [always] loves us and who [has once for all] freed us [or washed us] from our sins by His own blood (His sacrificial death). (Revelations 1:5 AMP)

This powerful truth gives every believer the confidence to live out that truth by faith. The blood of Jesus has paid the price for the unrighteous nature that every human being was born into. Henceforth, through Jesus Christ alone, we accept His righteous nature. But why do Christians find it hard to accept that we are justified through what Christ did? It's because of pride!

One thing that is very much needed for a believer is humility. God already knows who you are. There is no need to pretend or cover up anything else trying to paralyze you from releasing yourself—flaws and all. You need to *surrender it all.*

This is the key of how to enjoy the benefits of God's grace flowing in every area of your life. He told us in His Word He resists the proud, and He gives more grace to the humble.

It's so important to understand that if you are not willing to surrender all to Him, you will continue to be in control of the decisions you make in your life; it is inconsistent with the life of a Christian. Instead, we should desire for our lives to go in the direction consistent with His will. So, what does a humble Christian look like? Begin in sincerity.

> Grace and peace be multiplied unto you through the knowledge of God, and of Jesus our Lord, According as his divine power hath given unto us all things that pertain unto life and godliness, through the knowledge of him that hath called us to glory and virtue: Whereby are given unto us exceeding great and precious promises: that by these ye might be partakers of the divine nature, having escaped the corruption that is in the world through lust. And beside this, giving all diligence, add to your faith virtue; and to virtue knowledge; And to knowledge temperance; and to temperance patience; and to patience godliness; And to godliness brotherly kindness; and to brotherly kindness charity. For if these things be in you, and abound, they make you that ye shall neither be barren nor unfruitful in the knowledge of our Lord Jesus Christ. (2 Peter 1:2–8 KJV)

Here are a few items I believe will have a huge impact on your character:

- Let everything about you concentrate on what Jesus accomplished (His righteousness) and learn to worship Him.
- Choose to love.
- Pray for the Lord to create a passion in you, to say what is in His heart.
- Concentrate on the areas of improvement desired in your own walk. The Holy Spirit will minister to you throughout the day, remembering you are who He reveals about in His Word.
- Study the scriptures. Take notes. Record the thoughts the Holy Spirit places on your heart.
- Welcome a teachable spirit and receive correction from the Lord with gratitude.
- Be prayerful, be persistent, be patient.

These are small but big changes. Although it may seem like this approach is self-centered, it is far from it. You are training yourself how to be effective in the lives of others when you concentrate on the areas in your life needing progress. A believer needs to challenge himself daily by looking into the mirror of the Word. As you locate an area inconsistent with the fruit of the Spirit, you can adjust your attitude and pray concerning that area.

For example, if you are someone who grew up within a family of gossipers, it is feasible that you may have established some of those behaviors. A gossiper is someone who does not speak words of edification. They speak words that try to draw a person down.

Since you have located this area that is not mirroring who you are, the next action is to find the scripture(s) that speaks to you about what is in the Father's heart concerning the matter. I've listed three scriptures below to mirror our example on gossiping.

And since they did not see fit to acknowledge God or consider Him worth knowing [as their Creator], God gave them over to a depraved mind, to do things which are improper and repulsive, until they were filled (permeated, saturated) with every kind of unrighteousness, wickedness, greed, evil; full of envy, murder, strife, deceit, malice, and mean-spiritedness. They are gossips [spreading rumors]. (Romans 1:29, 30 AMP)

Now at the same time, they also learn to be idle as they go from house to house; and not only idle but also gossips and [b]busybodies [meddlers in things that do not concern them], talking about things they should not mention. (1 Timothy 5:13 AMP)

Do not let unwholesome [foul, profane, worthless, vulgar] words ever come out of your mouth, but only such speech as is good for building up others, according to the need (and) the occasion, so that it will be a blessing to those who hear [you speak]. (Ephesians 4:29 AMP)

Because you can see that the Word of God speaks against idle talk (gossip), you must learn how to adjust your mind-set and the way you carry a conversation. Pray that God will give you the wisdom during this transition phase. Remember, the flesh will not cooperate because you have changed. The Holy Spirit is helping you to renew your thoughts to think like Christ.

Again, I'd like to be clear: you can't have genuine change without the Holy Spirit. Whatever area you would like to see the change in needs supernatural intervention.

Henceforth, you will need to channel your prayers, confident in God's grace in the matter. Continuing with the example we are using concerning gossip, you may also need to avoid certain people for a while until you gather enough strength to hold your tongue. At the appointed time, the Holy Spirit will give you the courage to speak bold words of life into the conversation. Encourage yourself in the Lord by focusing on Jesus and His humility.

So, don't be trying to force change by "doing things" to gain God's favor. You will only bring frustration on yourself. You may wonder what I mean by *doing things*. The whole idea of humility has to do with your true intentions. I'll use Martha and Mary to illustrate my point. Once you read the scriptures below, you'll notice that Mary positioned herself at the Lord's feet to hear His teaching, while Martha was busy serving.

The concern is not so much that she was serving but more so her intentions while serving. She was trying to gain the approval of the Master by doing things. We can see it because she asks the Lord Jesus to scold Mary for "not doing anything." Jesus replied by saying it was Mary who was doing the one thing that was needed, which was to depend on His every word spoken.

> Now while they were on their way, Jesus entered a village [called Bethany], and a woman named Martha welcomed Him into her home. She had a sister named Mary, who seated herself at the Lord's feet and was continually listening to His teaching. But Martha was very busy and distracted with all of her serving responsibilities; and she approached Him and said, "Lord, is it of no concern to You that my sister has left me to do the serving alone? Tell her to help me and do her part." But the Lord replied to her, "Martha, Martha, you are worried and bothered and anxious about so many things; but only one thing is necessary, for Mary has chosen the good part [that which is to her advantage], which will not be taken away from her." (Luke 10:38–42 AMP)

Mary was aware that this was not an ordinary man who had entered their home. She took advantage of the opportunity to get whatever the Lord was willing to give. Mary laid her cares at the feet of Jesus. She fed on His thoughts. The eager student wanted to drink into the wells of living waters. Mary recognized the value in every word released from the lips of Jesus. She rested in His grace. Her posture suggested she counted herself inferior to Him.

Humility is counting your abilities impotent, inferior to the Lord's. Before God will build you up spiritually, carnal thinking has to be torn down, demolished. Martha couldn't see what she needed because she lacked the ability to discern the superiority in Jesus. Martha may have held Jesus in high regard but not the highest regard. Her efforts in trying to please the Lord Jesus were only distractions that discouraged her from being taught by Him.

Do you recall when the Lord recruited Peter and James? They were in the profession of catching fish. Luke recounted that day. In his account, Jesus told Peter and James to place their nets in the water to catch fish. Peter explained to Jesus that the probability of catching anything was zero. However, Peter lowered his net into the water as Jesus requested and gasped when he saw results of an overflow of fish. At that moment, Peter realized his weakness and the Lord's strength. He chose to follow Christ and become a fisher of men.

> When He, (Jesus), had finished speaking, He said to Simon [Peter], "Put out into the deep water and lower your nets for a catch [of fish]." Simon replied, "Master, we worked hard all night [to the point of exhaustion] and caught nothing [in our nets], but at Your word I will [do as you say and] lower the nets [again]." When they had done this, they caught a great number of fish, and their nets were [at the point of] breaking; so they signaled to their partners in the other boat to come and help them. And they came and filled both of the boats [with fish], so that they began to sink. But when Simon Peter saw this, he fell down at Jesus' knees, saying, "Go away from me, for I am a sinful man, O Lord!" For he and all his companions were completely astounded at the catch of fish which they had taken; and so were James and John, sons of Zebedee, who were partners with Simon [Peter].

> Jesus said to Simon, "Have no fear; from now on you will be catching men!" (Luke 5:4–10 AMP)

It is very dangerous to develop false confidence by believing God is so pleased with you because of your good deeds. Eventually, you will develop a self-righteous mentality. This mind-set will lead you to be a religious, know-it-all Christian feeling left behind. It's because you have fallen from grace, not because of any sin. You have pride issues. God said in His Word to work out your own salvation with fear and trembling. He's telling you to be conscious of your own relationship with Him.

> Have this same attitude in yourselves which was in Christ Jesus [look to Him as your example in selfless humility], who, although He existed in the form (and) unchanging essence of God [as One with Him, possessing the fullness of all the divine attributes—the entire nature of deity], did not regard equality with God a thing to be grasped or asserted [as if He did not already possess it, or was afraid of losing it]; but emptied Himself [without renouncing or diminishing His deity, but only temporarily giving up the outward expression of divine equality and His rightful dignity] by assuming the form of a bond-servant, and being made in the likeness of men [He became completely human but was without sin, being fully God and fully man]. (Philippians 2:5–7 AMP)
>
> But the fruit of the Spirit [the result of His presence within us] is love [unselfish concern for others], joy, [inner] peace, patience [not the ability to wait, but how we act while waiting], kindness, goodness, faithfulness, gentleness, self-control. Against such things there is no law. And those who belong to Christ Jesus have

crucified the [l]sinful nature together with its passions and appetites). (Galatian 5:22–24 AMP)

And if you have not yet received Christ, I pray that as God reveals Himself to you personally, or through a believer, or even through this book. I pray that you will respond to Him and receive the gift of eternal life.

CHAPTER 8

Unselfish Love

Grasp this. To love means to see as God sees and have the compassion that moves you to have mercy on top of mercy for anyone who is struggling with whatever battle has crushed them to the desperation of not knowing where to turn. A love that causes you to lift your head and raise your voice and cry out for that individual who is bleeding and hurting spiritually and physically. It has nothing to do with how many scriptures you know or how many church services you may have attended. It has everything to do with whether your heart is filled with His love. Because if you possess His love, you can't help but be merciful from within.

Paul put His life on the line repeatedly throughout the epistles. He had compassion for the people who didn't know Jesus and the ones ignorant of His grace. Our Lord had touched him in such a way he was so eager to take the gospel as far out as he could go. It is the Holy Spirit that changes a man/woman from the inside. It's not words spoken from the emotions of the senses but words that speak from the emotions of the Spirit of God that will cause an avalanche of tears of repentance.

Our God is jealous, and He wants *all* the glory to Him alone. Paul spoke of Jesus the entire time. He didn't speak of Himself. Even Jesus refused to reflect upon Himself, but He made it all about God. Our Lord was teaching us the mind-set of being a willing and obedient servant. See the scripture below:

> "For I have come down from heaven, not to do My own will, but to do the will of Him who sent Me. This is the will of Him who sent Me, that of all that He has given Me I lose nothing, but that I [give new life and] raise it up at the last day. For this is My Father's will and purpose, that everyone who sees the Son and believes in Him [as Savior] will have eternal life, and I will raise him up [from the dead] on the last day." (John 6:38–40 AMP)

Pride is a spirit, and it is not of God. Its fruits are division and self-centered behaviors. Jesus has torn down the wall of division and has opened all His merciful and abounding grace. This means that Jesus has given every individual on this earth access into His kingdom by faith in Him. Too many Christians emphasize trying to determine whether or not someone is a Christian. There are false prophets who have altered the teachings of the Bible to serve their needs; this is not whom I am referring to. Such cases are wicked altogether and must answer to God.

I am speaking about the young man that gave his life to Christ a few months ago and is still struggling with an addiction of some sort. His parents had been praying that God would touch him supernaturally and provoke him to change his path. This young man prays to God from his heart. But despite his struggles of trying to be a good Christian, he finds himself challenged and wanting to go back to old habits.

Friends and family only add fuel to the fire as they remind him of how badly he is doing. The words that are meant to encourage change only produce harm. The mother quickly forgets, unintentionally, that it was God who caused him to fall on his knees and cry out in the first place. And it is this same God who is able to make him stand.

This was one of the challenges for my father. He loved the Lord. However, for many years, he tried to please Him in his own strength and knowledge, just as I did. This grew tiresome for him. His motives were good, but he wasn't familiar with receiving the blessings that God had for him by grace. He wrestled with self-righteousness. As he matured in life, he learned to love the Word of God more and more. As he grew closer to his departure from earth, he gained a greater revelation of God's decision to choose to favor and love him despite himself, as did I. He spoke prophecies, and I saw them come to pass, even to this day. Such an amazing, patient, and compassionate God we serve.

Let's look at King David's struggles as a king who had so much at his leisure. He cried out to God in repentance when he gained a revelation of how much he had offended God when he committed adultery and murder. He had been raised a shepherd boy, under the laws of Moses, from the tribe of Judah. He was trained in the things of God according to the Hebrew customs. He was taught to believe that God truly had His chosen prophets that spoke to a man on His behalf. And most importantly, he believed that he was God's anointed. In other words, David was conscious of the truth that God had witnessed his actions. He loved the Lord and was troubled about how he had offended Him.

We must allow others to come to that revelation as God reveals it to them. Once he/she understands what it means to be a child of God, a switch has already gone off inside, and change immediately follows. However, with everything, there are stages. A born-again Christian is a baby in the spirit realm. There are baby hiccups that will happen. We must be patient and allow God to do what only He can. And if He does choose to use you to speak a word to that person, correct in love, *gently*.

Below is an event that occurred under the covenant of the law. The Israelites had just settled in a city called Shittim. This account will give you a greater appreciation for the grace that we have received from Christ. They started having affairs with foreign women. They were known as Moabites. God told the Israelites that they could not be with these women. Instead, the Israelites slept with the women and participated in their satanic rituals of idol worshipping and eating foods sacrificed to their god, Baal.

This angered the Lord, so He ordered Moses to kill all the participating leaders in broad daylight as an example. The Lord wanted everyone in the congregation to witness and be aware of His disgust toward them.

In stupidity, one of the Israelites brought a pagan woman to his family in front of the prophet Moses. This was not only treason but also considered arrogance. Moses was highly regarded as a man of God. Phinehas, Aaron's grandson, was outraged by his brother's disobedience and took a spear and thrust it through both the man and the woman. God was pleased with Phinehas's quick action of obedience and his reverence toward God's anger. As a result, the Israelites were spared, and furthermore, God extended a covenant of peace to Phinehas and his descendants. You can read the full account in the book of Numbers, chapter 25.

Again, this was all under the old covenant. However, because of Jesus Christ, whom the Lord poured His wrath upon at the cross as a punishment for the sins of the entire world, every believer receives His (Jesus's) status of righteous by God's grace, given as a gift.

> For the Law was given through Moses, but grace [the unearned, undeserved favor of God] and truth came through Jesus Christ. (John 1:17 AMP)

Consciousness of God's grace may be the most challenging aspect of being a child of God. Many Christians do not know how to live life in the purposeful mind-set that he is righteous in Christ Jesus. Does this mean the believer can do whatever he wants? Of course not! A true believer will want to do what is in the Father's heart. As I stated in previous chapters, the Father's heart is found in His Word.

However, you will make wrong choices as you are developing in spiritual growth. Fortunately, we have the privilege of speaking directly to our Father. If we offend Him, He has given us our Lord Jesus as an advocate. So, we can pray to the Father knowing He cares for us. We are grateful that He has made a way for us to escape eternal separation from Him. Immediately, we repent and receive forgiveness because of the love we know He has for us and the love we have for Him.

So, don't be so quick to thrust the javelin into someone whom God is doing a work in. Jesus paid the price for their sins. I am not suggesting that anyone condone sin; the Lord hates sin, but he loves the individual who committed the act. Extend the same grace extended toward you. It is the Holy Spirit's ministry to teach and guide him, not you. This is a process that has to undergo stages.

Our part as believers is to pray. Jesus said to watch and pray. This is one of the things He was talking about. You may have witnessed a sister's behavior inconsistent with a believer. I caution you on how you approach the situation. Have you fallen on your knees and taken those concerns before God in love? Because if you sincerely want to affect her life, you will take it in prayer and then allow the Holy Spirit to guide your actions.

The scripture says do not put new wine in an old wineskin. The wine represents covenant. The old covenant has no part in the new covenant. Salvation can only come from the new covenant. We are all included. The covenant of God's grace is only through the Gospel of our Lord Jesus, who is the true light. The old covenant was only a shadow of what was to come.

> For the Law was given through Moses, but grace [the unearned, undeserved favor of God] and truth came through Jesus Christ. (John 1:17 AMP)

CHAPTER 9

Embedded Purpose

Let's continue. Around ten years of age, I was a member of the Catholic faith. I came home from my catechism class. They gave me a pamphlet about the story of Adam and Eve. The nun instructed me to discuss the pamphlet with my parents. I felt truly inspired by the story, but somehow, I felt there just had to be more to what I had read.

My dad was playing records in our living room as I shared it with him. He reached for a thick book with a black cover titled Holy Bible. He smacked the book with an open hand as it lay on the table and said, "This is what you need to read, not that." I was so privileged to read such a big book with so many pages. He reassured me I could have full access to it no matter what time of the day.

As a little child, I assumed my father had read and understood everything there was to know about the Bible, and most likely I had a lot of catching up to do. Eventually, I would come to learn that my dad, at that point in his life, didn't know how to commit himself to God's Word. I struggled, desperately trying to understand the "thous" the "arents" and "yehs" in the King James Version Bible.

I had no one to explain why God had made it so complicated for anyone to understand Him. It's funny how ignorant I was back then, but it's not unusual for many Christians. Strangely, although I believed in God, I didn't know Him, nor did I have a revelation of who Jesus was. I made no confession of Jesus being Lord of my life. I didn't know it was required. I didn't even understand salvation. How could I have appreciated Jesus Christ as the Son of God? My mother took me and my siblings to the Catholic church, but there was nothing during the services that ministered the love of Jesus or salvation.

Thankfully, God is merciful. He opened avenues of resources to help me to know Him. Years later, men and women came in and out of my life sporadically, explaining scriptures. Eventually, this increased my awareness and led me to receive Jesus into my heart with understanding. Today, I love the Word of God, and I have a passion to share what I have learned. The Lord has blessed me with undeserved testimonies that have charted my relationship with Him to higher dimensions.

This reminds me of Jeremiah the prophet. He was only twenty years old when God spoke to him. It amazed Jeremiah! God told him He would use him to be His voice. The young boy was afraid. His human impulse caused him to consider his inadequacies. Understandably, he measured himself against the religious leaders of the Jewish community. Why would highly qualified Levitical priests listen to him? These men dedicated years to searching scriptures and practicing the laws. Why would they pay attention to a boy who had little experience of the real world and its issues?

However, the Lord planned to give Jeremiah the confidence necessary to speak in the hostile environment awaiting him. He told Jeremiah that He had consecrated him for Himself. Jeremiah learned the traditions of the Levitical priesthood from his father and forefathers. His training began early, even though he didn't know it. This knowledge was beneficial, but God had even bigger plans for Jeremiah. God called him to be His prophet. The Lord gave Jeremiah the supernatural courage to proclaim His anointed word that could cost him his life.

How could this be that God would call upon such a young man to speak on His behalf? Was it even possible for the immature, unskilled boy to be taken seriously by the prominent leaders of the Jewish community? Only when the Holy Spirit is speaking through him. As you study the scriptures below, you will learn that the Lord God told Jeremiah that He had no reason to consider any of those weaknesses because He would be with him every step of the way.

Observe the following scriptures:

> Now the word of the Lord came to me, saying, "Before I formed you in the womb I knew you [and approved of you as My chosen instrument], And before you were born I consecrated you [to Myself as My own]; I have appointed you as a prophet to the nations." Then I said, "Ah, Lord God! Behold, I do not know how to speak, For I am [only] a young man." But the Lord said to me, "Do not say, 'I am [only] a young man,' Because everywhere I send you, you shall go, And whatever I command you, you shall speak. "Do not be afraid of them [or their hostile faces], For I am with you [always] to protect you and deliver you," says the Lord. Then the Lord stretched out His hand and touched my mouth, and the Lord said to me, "Behold (hear Me), I have put My words in your mouth. (Jeremiah 1:4–9 AMP)

You may say, "But what does that have to do with me?" It has plenty to do with you. Having a physical body on this earth qualifies you to have something to do with this. In this world, man has developed methods of existing on this earth progressively. Examples would include creating unique living quarters, hunting skills for food and apparel, and utilizing plants for food and medicines.

Those were ideas planted in their spirits by the Creator of all things. This is how we eventually discover our purpose. But the Lord meant each purpose to be to the glory of Jesus and not to the glory of self. Our life on earth is progressive because of the things the Lord reveals to us. The "creative inventions" were already in existence; God hid them until the appointed time.

> In the beginning [before all-time] was the Word (Christ), and the Word was with God, and [b]the Word was God Himself. He was [continually existing] in the beginning [co-eternally] with God. All things were made and came

> into existence through Him; and without Him not even
> one thing was made that has come into being. (John
> 1:1–4 AMP)

God used Jeremiah to proclaim His anger toward the disobedience of Judah (Israelites from the same tribe as David). He told them they needed to repent from the widespread evil act of worshipping idols. The Lord loved Judah, despite their behaviors, and that was why He selected Jeremiah to warn them. In verse 2, Jeremiah tells God of his weaknesses of being an adolescent. The Lord reassures him by telling him He will be with him during the challenging journey. Isn't this encouraging for the life of a believer?

According to the New Testament, the Lord has chosen every believer to warn the lost to receive the gift of salvation in Jesus Christ now. Jeremiah tried to imagine himself speaking words of condemnation to men who were much older, wiser, and more educated than he was. This only caused him to feel afraid and incapable. But the Lord God encouraged him, saying He would put the words he should speak in his mouth.

As believers, we allow the Lord to speak through us powerfully when we submit to Him. The constant flow of that ability to hear and preach the good news is empowerment by the infilling of the Holy Spirit (book of Acts, chapters 1 and 2). Jeremiah preached condemnation. The believer preaches forgiveness and eternal salvation. This is the grace of God. It is His love that leads sinners to repentance.

The power of God inside of a true believer unleashes miracle-working power when he acts out in faith. It changes this individual into another man. The more he preaches salvation, the stronger he becomes from his innermost being. That happened with Jeremiah. He transformed more and more into the man that the Lord had purposed him to be.

Let's look at Joseph, Abraham's grandson. At seventeen years old, he dreamed dreams that positioned him over his family. In his immature stage, he could not discern the meaning of the dreams. These dreams provoked his brothers to become so enraged with him they sold him into slavery to the Ishmaelites, who took him into Egypt.

So Jacob (Israel) lived in the land [a]where his father [Isaac] had been a stranger (sojourner, resident alien), in the land of Canaan. These are the generations of Jacob. Joseph, when he was seventeen years old, was shepherding the flock with his brothers [Dan, Naphtali, Gad, and Asher]; the boy was with the sons of Bilhah and Zilpah, his father's [[b]secondary] wives; and Joseph brought back a bad report about them to their father. Now Israel (Jacob) loved Joseph more than all his children, because he was the son of his old age; and he made him a [distinctive] [c]multicolored tunic. His brothers saw that their father loved Joseph more than all of his brothers; so they hated him and could not [find it within themselves to] speak to him on friendly terms. Now Joseph dreamed a dream, and he told it to his brothers, and they [d]hated him even more. He said to them, "Please listen to [the details of] this dream which I have dreamed; we [brothers] were binding sheaves [of grain stalks] in the field, and lo, my sheaf [suddenly] got up and stood upright and remained standing; and behold, your sheaves stood all around my sheaf and bowed down [in respect]." His brothers said to him, "Are you actually going to reign over us? Are you really going to rule and govern us as your subjects?" So they hated him even more for [telling them about] his dreams and for his [arrogant] words.

But Joseph dreamed still another dream, and told it to his brothers [as well]. He said, "See here, I have again dreamed a dream, and lo, [this time I saw] eleven stars and the sun and the moon bowed down [in respect] to me!" He told it to his father as well as to his brothers; but his father rebuked him and said to him [in disbelief], "What is [the meaning of] this dream that you have dreamed? Shall I and your mother and your brothers actually come to bow down to the ground [in respect] before you?" Joseph's brothers were envious and jealous of him, but his father kept the words [of Joseph] in mind [wondering about their meaning]. Then his brothers went to pasture their father's flock near Shechem. Israel (Jacob) said to Joseph, "Are not your brothers pasturing [the flock] at Shechem? Come, and I will send you to them." And he said, "Here I am [ready to obey you]." Then Jacob said to him, "Please go and see whether everything is all right with your brothers and all right with the flock; then bring word [back] to me." So he sent him from the Hebron Valley, and he went to Shechem. Now a certain man found Joseph, and saw that he was wandering around and had lost his way in the field; so the man asked him, "What are you looking for?" He said, "I am looking for my brothers. Please tell me where they are pasturing our flocks." Then the man said, "[They were here, but] they have moved on from this place. I heard them say, 'Let us go to [e]Dothan.'" So Joseph went after his brothers and found them at Dothan.

And when they saw him from a distance, even before he came close to them, they plotted to kill him. They said to one another, "Look, here comes this [f]dreamer. Now then, come and let us kill him and throw him into one of the [g]pits (cisterns, underground water storage); then we will say [to our father], 'A wild animal killed and devoured him'; and we shall see what will become of his dreams!" Now Reuben [the eldest] heard this and rescued him from their hands and said, "Let us not take his life." Reuben said to them, "Do not shed his blood, but [instead] throw him [alive] into the pit that is here in the wilderness, and do not lay a hand on him [to kill him]"—[he said this so] that he could rescue him from them and return him [safely] to his father. Now when Joseph reached his brothers, they stripped him of his tunic, the [distinctive] [h]multicolored tunic which he was wearing; then they took him and threw him into the pit. Now the pit was empty; there was no water in it.

Then they sat down to eat their meal. When they looked up, they saw a caravan of [i]Ishmaelites coming from Gilead [east of the Jordan], with their camels bearing ladanum resin [for perfume] and balm and [j] myrrh, going on their way to carry the cargo down to Egypt. Judah said to his brothers, "What do we gain if we kill our brother and cover up his blood (murder)? Come, let us [instead] sell him to these Ishmaelites [and [k]Midianites] and not lay our hands on him, because he is our brother and our flesh." So his brothers listened to him and agreed. Then as the [l]Midianite [and Ishmaelite] traders were passing by, the brothers pulled Joseph up and lifted him out of the pit, and they sold him to the Ishmaelites for twenty shekels of silver. And so they took Joseph [as a captive] into Egypt.

Now Reuben [unaware of what had happened] returned to the pit, and [to his great alarm found that] Joseph was not in the pit; so he tore his clothes [in deep sorrow]. He rejoined his brothers and said, "The boy is not there; as for me, where shall I go [to hide from my father]?" Then they took Joseph's tunic, slaughtered a male goat and dipped the tunic in the blood; and they brought the multicolored tunic to their father, saying, "We have found this; please examine it and decide whether or not it is your son's tunic." He recognized it and said, "It is my son's tunic. A wild animal has devoured him; Joseph is without doubt torn in pieces!" So Jacob tore his clothes [in grief], put [m]on sackcloth and mourned many days for his son. Then all his sons and daughters attempted to console him, but he refused to be comforted and said, "I will go down to Sheol (the place of the dead) in mourning for my son." And his father wept for him. Meanwhile, in Egypt the Midianites sold Joseph [as a slave] to Potiphar, an officer of Pharaoh and the captain of the [royal] guard. (Genesis 37 AMP)

Now let's briefly analyze David's journey. He was a shepherd boy who guarded his sheep with his life. David had extraordinary skills in the wilderness and a great love for his sheep. The Bible records he took the life of a bear and a lion to protect his sheep.

The ordinary person would not recognize those qualities as training mechanisms to lead an army or rule over a selected group of God's creation. But the wisdom of God reveals it plainly.

One day, the prophet Samuel goes to Bethlehem and instructs Jesse (David's father) and his sons to consecrate themselves and join him for a sacrifice. His intentions were to anoint the next king that would rule over the children of Israel. The Bible records that Samuel examined each of the sons according to external appearance. However, none of the men were God's chosen. Samuel discovered that God selected David, the youngest and least likely.

Strategically, the Lord positioned David to fight a fierce opponent, a giant by the name of Goliath. This giant was a member of the Philistine army. The Israelites were afraid of them. Goliath underestimated David's potential; so did Saul and his army. However, David's confidence in the power of God caused him to defeat Goliath with one blow to the head. The Israelites won the war, and David had become a member of King Saul's army.

After Saul's death, David was recognized as the new king. He was not innocent in his deeds as a king; however, in every wrong decision, he repented from his heart and prayed to God, whom he knew heard him and loved him. He believed that God was responsible for every good thing in his life. He was grateful. He remembered that God had a great purpose for his life. David felt grieved because of his offenses against his God who loved him so. And he was wise to know that the Lord forgave him.

The Lord purposely chose the lineage of King David to usher in our Lord Jesus. The plans that the Lord had for David were greater than he could comprehend. The gentle, caring little boy who loved the vulnerable sheep was a fierce lion who would defend the sheep quicker than the blink of an eye. That is the shadowing of the true Savior to come: King Jesus!

David fought with physical weapons that defeated his enemies and gave his people temporary peace. Our Lord Jesus Christ defeated the enemy behind all the manifestations of darkness by willfully laying down His life in innocence, all to defeat the spiritual death that the first man, Adam, had accepted on behalf of all mankind. And now, we who are alive in Christ have eternal life, eternal peace, and eternal joy!

God chose Joseph, Jeremiah, and David at their youthful stages in life. Each was undergoing training without realizing that the things they were becoming proficient in were only part of what God would use them to do. They appeared to be unqualified in the eyes of man. But God, who is able to do abundantly more than we can ask or think, revealed His power through the miracles He performed in each of their lives.

Allow God to build you. Decide that He is Lord and that He has a purpose designed for you. Be conscious of His grace over your life. Be thankful for everything that you do. Walk in love. If you become boastful, proud, jealous, anxious, or easily angered, take a minute to humble yourself before God, as I discussed earlier. Know that those behaviors are not who you are and realize that you are growing. Ask God to teach you how to be patient and content and how to love. Don't be discouraged. Be attentive to your day-to-day actions by focusing on those areas where the Lord God is training you in. Select a scripture for that area and meditate on it throughout the day.

You may hear words spoken to you, or a nudge in your spirit, or someone He sends to relay a message. Just always know that you are in Christ, and His Spirit now lives in you. Your means of communication is not the source you once looked to. You are a child of God. That means you are declared holy (separated for God's purpose) and accepted by Him. You are not blamable, and you are righteous and full of His glory, even when you are disappointed in wrong choices. You can sincerely apologize and start over. It is only by His grace. "In all these things, you are more than conquerors." So, no matter what trials come, and they will come, remember those words.

CHAPTER 10

The Father, the Son, and the Holy Spirit Are One

In 1992, I concluded that there was too much controversy regarding what I read in the Bible versus what the Catholic faith had taught me. I abandoned that faith and continued my Bible studies from home. I listened to the teachings of a distinguished pastor on television. He seemed to use a lot of biblical scriptures while teaching the members of his congregation. He used the name of Jesus frequently while addressing his members, as though he was proving his case in a court of law. I was inspired, and this motivated me, even more, to want to know Jesus.

I would ask myself, "Do I know Jesus?" I had read about Him being the Son of God, but I was not sure how to acknowledge Him without offending the Father. As for the existence of the Holy Spirit, I avoided that portion altogether. The Old Testament said that God was a jealous God and that I should acknowledge only Him. But then the New Testament said that God could accept no one except through Jesus Christ; everything appeared to be conflicting. Which was right? The answer is that they are both true. The Father, the Son, and the Holy Spirit is a mystery that the wisdom of God has hidden since the days of the Old Testament (as stated in the book of Hebrews), but God reveals it in the New Testament through Christ Jesus!

As I share more of my personal experiences in this chapter, I would like to introduce you to a fresh way of worshipping the Lord through the knowledge and revelation of who He truly is. He is one God existing in three persons. You may have accepted that statement into your mind but never really searched the scriptures to appreciate how beneficial it is to you as a Christian. Perhaps it's because you were afraid of admitting that you have those questions secretly hidden inside of you. But I have good news! The Lord wants you to question, search, and find the truth through His Word.

Observe the scriptures below. It is a prayer for believers who have received Jesus as their personal Savior but lack spiritual knowledge. The purpose of having the spiritual knowledge is to know the Lord through His revealed Word He gives to those who desire Him.

> [I always pray] that the God of our Lord Jesus Christ, the Father of glory, may grant you a spirit of wisdom and of revelation [that gives you a deep and personal and intimate insight] into the true knowledge of Him [for we know the Father through the Son]. And [I pray] that the eyes of your heart [the very center and core of your being] may be enlightened [flooded with light by the Holy Spirit], so that you will know and cherish the hope [the divine guarantee, the confident expectation] to which He has called you, the riches of His glorious inheritance in the saints (God's people), and [so that you will begin to know] what the immeasurable and unlimited and surpassing greatness of His [active, spiritual] power is in us who believe. (Ephesians 1:17–19 AMP)

One early Saturday morning, a carpenter knocked at my door to perform a few scheduled repairs. He noticed I had been reading the Bible and tested my understanding. "How do you pray?" he asked. I didn't understand his question. Why would he ask me how is it I pray? I pray the prayers taught from childhood, the "Our Father" prayer. I had decided when I left the Catholic faith I would no longer take part in the rosary by praying to Mary.

So, the carpenter continued by asking me who I specifically speak to when I pray. Expecting this was some trick question meant to minimize my understanding of the Bible, reluctantly I answered that I pray to the Father. He challenged me by asking in whose authority am I able to go to the Father. His words were frustrating. He was a senior man, and I was trying my best to be respectful and patient. I said confidently that I go with the authority of being a child of God. So, he countered by saying that I cannot pray directly to the Father and that I should go through Jesus, and He will relay my words to the Father.

He badgered me by saying I did not know Jesus and therefore I did not know God. I grabbed my Bible and pointed out several scriptures in the Old Testament to support my belief. "Jesus is the Son, and I love Him, but I fellowship directly with God," I exclaimed to the carpenter. I told him of my childhood years and how I had been speaking with God since I was about nine years old.

"I spoke to the Lord every day," I explained. "And I truly believe that God was listening." The old man concluded within himself that it was of no use. He realized I supposedly had all the answers, and he decided to allow me to remain in my ignorance because I would not give him my ear.

Now, the old man believed that a Christian should pray to Jesus, which is unscriptural. But he caused me to reevaluate my understanding of the Trinity. So, that evening as I opened my Bible, I felt different. My confidence was lacking in whether I was right about praying to the Father. I shrugged off the uncomfortable feeling, closed my Bible, and fell asleep convincing myself that I was right and he was just confused (he was wrong in doctrine, but his heart was sincerely in the right place).

Two months had gone by, and I still could not shake this nagging feeling of, *What if I am wrong?* I recalled how the old man had shared several testimonies of how he almost died on three different occasions, but calling on the name of Jesus had rescued him. He said it was because of his relationship with Jesus that he had developed over the years. I was finally willing to listen to the old man as I rehearsed his words in my memory.

I sat on my bedroom floor and went into meditation. I told God that it was because of the love I had for Him that I would allow my heart to receive the truth and that I needed Him to help me learn how to love

Jesus without offending Him. So, I said, "Jesus, I want to know You and truly love You." I meditated on what Jesus did for me on the cross. Finally, in tears of desperation, I said in faith, "Jesus, you are my Lord. I cannot go to the Father, except through You. Teach me to know You. Show me how to relate to You without offending God."

What were my intentions? Why did I cry out in tears? It's because I wanted more of God. I wanted Him to know that I was willing to step outside of the things I thought I knew and instead embrace what He knew. I wasn't sure what that looked like, but I was willing to allow Him to teach me. I felt a sense of emptiness, and I couldn't locate the root of my problem.

I strategized, and ultimately, I focused on readings the New Testament portion of the Bible. I believed that if I could read everything that Jesus said, I would be more likely to get to know Him. Looking back at that period of my life, I realize that God had opened my heart to the truth: I had not accepted Jesus Christ as Lord and Savior of my life. The Lord had used the old man to lead me to Christ. Although I was ignorant of what it meant to be saved, my greatest desire was to have an authentic relationship with Jesus Christ and God with no confusion. Years later, I learned that God truly is my Father and that I am unquestionably His child. He has approved me through the blood of Jesus Christ.

> He predestined and lovingly planned for us to be adopted to Himself as [His own] children through Jesus Christ, in accordance with the kind intention and good pleasure of His will. (Ephesians 1:5 AMP)

Now, I wish to dig a little deeper into the relationship between the Father and the Son. God is God alone. However, His existence is in three persons, as I mentioned earlier. The beginning of the Bible is not the beginning of everything; it is the beginning of time. God created time as a tool for His creation on earth, as a means of measurement to distinguish seasons. He considers anything outside of the natural realm of time eternity.

This natural realm has a temporary status; therefore, it is only wise to discern and use time wisely. The significance of acknowledging the realm of eternity and the realm of the natural (temporary) is that it will enhance your vision of how God sees as you study His written Word.

First, God is a Spirit. He created Adam and breathed His Spirit into Adam, and then Adam, who was initially dirt, became alive. This life was eternal life because it was God's breath inside of His creation. The book of Genesis continues to inform us that God also created the first woman, whom Adam named Eve. The devil deceives them because of their unwillingness to trust God. Their act of disobedience delivered them into the hands of the enemy, and immediately they became tainted.

> Then God said, "Let Us (Father, Son, Holy Spirit) make man in Our image, according to Our likeness [not physical, but a spiritual personality and moral likeness]; and let them have complete authority over the fish of the sea, the birds of the air, the cattle, and over the entire earth, and over everything that creeps and crawls on the earth." (Genesis 1:26 AMP)

God threw the two out of the garden, and the earth was now cursed. This fallen state of the earth changed the dynamics of governing for all creation. God initially gave man authority over everything on the planet, even the enemy, but now the devil had stolen that privilege. I urge you to revisit the book of Genesis, chapters 1 through 4. I will expound more a little later in the chapter.

The significance of Adam's disobedience sheds light on believing that God did physically enter this dark world as the man Jesus. Scriptures tell us that there are three witnesses in heaven to support this truth: the Father, the Word, and the Holy Ghost.

> For there are three that bear record in heaven, the Father, the Word, and the Holy Ghost: and there three are one. (1 John 5:7 KJV)

Note that the second person is the Word. The Word is Jesus Christ!

> And the Word (Christ) became flesh, and lived among us; and we [actually] saw His glory, glory as belongs to the [One and] only begotten *Son* of the Father, [the Son who is truly unique, the only One of His kind, who is] full of grace and truth (absolutely free of deception). (John 1:14 AMP)

Henceforth, the Word is alive. This is the life that gives life to the dead in spirit. The emptiness I felt inside of me was the absence of Jesus. Having a relationship with the Father bypassing His Son is impossible. It was the sincerity of my heart that caused me to trust that the Bible was the ultimate truth. Therefore, as I read the Bible, receptive to believing that Jesus and God were one, I experienced a real change inside of me. I didn't know it then, but I was eating the bread of life.

> Jesus answered them and said, Verily, verily, I say unto you, Ye seek me, not because ye saw the miracles, but because ye did eat of the loaves, and were filled. Labour not for the meat which perisheth, but for that meat which endureth unto everlasting life, which the Son of man shall give unto you: for him hath God the Father sealed. (John 6: 26–27 KJV)

Did you see that! God the Father has authorized and put the seal on Jesus to give us the eternal food that only He can give—His Word. Even though I could not articulate the thoughts that my mind was experiencing, I instinctively knew that a light inside of me was removing the dark fog of confusion. The Bible says that Jesus is the light of the world. He is God's spoken word, exposing lies and revealing the truth.

I want to continue a little further on the discussion of Jesus as the spoken Word of God, who is the eternal food for the spirit of a believer. In the previous scriptures, the people had been searching for Jesus. He told them they were more concerned with what He could give to them for their temporary needs as opposed to what they needed for eternal security.

After the Lord Jesus scolded them, the people requested that He should tell them exactly what they needed to do to work for God. He answered plainly by saying that they should believe in the one that God sent—Him (Jesus). God *sent* His Word in the form of a man who is His Son.

In the thirtieth verse, the Jews decided that in order for them to believe anything that Jesus said to them, He needed to give them a sign similar to what the prophets of old had done, such as Moses, when God caused manna (bread) to fall from the sky as he fed the Hebrews in the wilderness. In their ignorance and double-mindedness, the Jewish people asked the Lord for a sign even though they had just witnessed the miracle of Jesus multiplying five loaves of bread and two fish, which miraculously fed over five thousand people. They also declared Him the promised prophet!

> When the people saw the sign (attesting miracle) that He had done, they began saying, "This is without a doubt the promised Prophet who is to come into the world!" (John 6:14 AMP)

Their words confirmed what the Lord Jesus spoke when he told them they were only concerned about their bellies. He continued to explain to them that the bread they were referring to during Moses's lifetime was temporary bread. That manna had an expiration date and was purposed to turn, spoil, and produce maggots. However, the true bread that came down from heaven gave eternal life to all who ate it.

> Then Jesus said unto them, Verily, verily, I say unto you, Moses gave you not that bread from heaven; but my

> Father giveth you the true bread from heaven. For the bread of God is he which cometh down from heaven, and giveth life unto the world. (John 6:32–33 KJV)

As you continue reading these scriptures, you learn that the Hebrews persisted and asked Jesus for tangible evidence. They could not discern rightly because their hearts focused only on themselves.

Confusion happens when people with the wrong motives read the Bible. If you want to receive anything from God, it must be by the faith that believes everything written in the Bible is true. Even if you don't understand it yet, you must receive it just as an infant dependent on the breast milk of his mother. The child sucks the milk with no doubt that the milk will provide the essential nutrients for his life.

If you want to press forward in your desire to know God, first be honest enough to admit your ignorance and then look to the Word. Remember to establish within yourself, by faith, that the Word of God has final authority over your life. It is not a sign of weakness but a concrete measure of spiritual growth. Many of the Pharisees and Sadducees had a know-it-all mentality. Jesus told them because you say you see, (or in other words, you think you know better), your sin remains. It does not differ from the parable He spoke when He said that it is easier for a camel to pass through the eye of a needle than it is for a rich man to be saved.

The rich man believed that his money could purchase all of his needs. His greed swallowed him up and yielded him a false sense of security. The things from the natural realm cannot produce the spiritual fruit of life because they are spiritually corrupt. The scripture I've posted from Hebrews highlights the effectiveness of how God's Word can determine the sincerity of an individual's heart.

> For the word of God is living and active and full of power [making it operative, energizing, and effective]. It is sharper than any two-edged [b]sword, penetrating as far as the division of the [c]soul and spirit [the completeness of a person], and of both joints and marrow

[the deepest parts of our nature], exposing and judging the very thoughts and intentions of the heart. (Hebrews 4:12 AMP)

Hopefully, you have received some clarity concerning the relationship that exists with the Father and the Son as one God, in the person of the Father, and the person of the Son who is the Father's spoken Word. But there is still so much more to share. The book of John and Genesis, chapter 1, unleash divine revelations that open our hearts to the deity of God the Father, Son, and Holy Spirit. I will show you these fascinating discoveries. But first, allow me to impart knowledge on the person of God's Spirit.

The Ministry of the Holy Spirit

How beautiful it is to live a life that is pleasing to God.

But still, how do you continue when you are feeling overwhelmed?

How do you demonstrate it consistently in your life?

How do your actions reflect your belief?

What mentality should you have without feeling frustrated?

Paul spoke about this in Romans, chapter 7. He said the things he does not want to do, he ends up doing them. But the things he wants to do, he does not do them. What was Paul referencing? He was exploring the fleshy thoughts of understanding how to please God. In your strength, with your thoughts, you cannot please God.

The spirit is willing but the flesh is weak. (Matthew 26:41 AMP)

Let's get a clearer understanding of what is considered flesh in the Bible. The flesh is anything that is connected to the natural realm and its way of thinking. Your physical body is connected to the natural realm. It is not who you are. It acts as a container or vessel that carries you.

Your body reflects its appearance based on genetics that have physical characteristics, mostly stemming from the family line you were born into, such as your hair color, skin complexion, facial structures, and so forth.

Also, be on guard by knowing that the flesh is not only the tangible things mentioned above; your thoughts are equally considered to be fleshy if they are inconsistent with God's Word. The five senses of a human being are tools used to relate to the natural realm. When a Christian relies solely on these senses, it can cause wrong decision-making. The five senses, which are see, smell, taste, touch, and hear, are easily susceptible to being manipulated by the enemy because he banks on believers and nonbelievers trusting in these human forms of understanding as concrete evidence.

However, you are a spirit being. When you entered this earth, it was by the initiation of human actions. You were born into the imprisonment of spiritual death because of Adam's sin. Therefore, you were born into corruption. The only way to escape the penalty of Adam's sin is to receive eternal life that comes only through Jesus Christ. Review the scripture posted below.

> Therefore, just as sin came into the world through one man, and death through sin, so death spread to all people [no one being able to stop it or escape its power], because they all sinned. Sin was [committed] in the world before the Law [was given], but sin is not charged [against anyone] when there is no law [against it]. Yet death ruled [over mankind] from Adam to Moses [the Lawgiver], even over those who had not sinned [c] as Adam did. Adam is a type of Him (Christ) who was to come [but in reverse—Adam brought destruction, Christ brought salvation]. (Romans 5:16–17 AMP)

The power of the blood of Jesus Christ has redeemed the believer from the disease that death held over God's creation. The flesh is equivalent to darkness and error. These characteristics are the nature of the devil. So, as Christians, we cannot trust the advice that comes from the natural realm; it's flawed. We need to train ourselves to inspect everything against the Word of God. Why? Because our emotions will try their best to influence our choices, and those feelings are not always truthful.

These are the passages from the book of Romans, chapter 7, that demonstrate the spiritual conflict that exists between the natural (carnal) and spiritual.

We know that the Law is spiritual, but I am a creature of the flesh [worldly, self-reliant—carnal and unspiritual], sold into slavery to sin [and serving under its control]. For I do not understand my own actions [I am baffled and bewildered by them]. I do not practice what I want to do, but I am doing the very thing I hate [and yielding to my human nature, my worldliness—my sinful capacity]. Now if I habitually do what I do not want to do, [that means] I agree with the Law, confessing that it is good (morally excellent). So now [if that is the case, then] it is no longer I who do it [the disobedient thing which I despise], but the sin [nature] which lives in me. For I know that nothing good lives in me, that is, in my flesh [my human nature, my worldliness—my sinful capacity]. For the willingness [to do good] is present in me, but the doing of good is not. For the good that I want to do, I do not do, but I practice the very evil that I do not want. But if I am doing the very thing I do not want to do, I am no longer the one doing it [that is, it is not me that acts], but the sin [nature] which lives in me.

So I find it to be the law [of my inner self], that evil is present in me, the one who wants to do good. For I joyfully delight in the law of God in my inner self [with my new nature], but I see a different law and rule of action in the members of my body [in its appetites and desires], waging war against the law of my mind and

> subduing me and making me a prisoner of the law of sin which is within my members. Wretched and miserable man that I am! Who will [rescue me and] set me free from this body of death [this corrupt, mortal existence]? Thanks be to God [for my deliverance] through Jesus Christ our Lord! So then, on the one hand I myself with my mind serve the law of God, but on the other, with my flesh [my human nature, my worldliness, my sinful capacity—I serve] the law of sin. (Romans 7:14–25 AMP)

Hopefully, you can pinpoint areas in your life that have been guided by the flesh. Recognizing them is key to being free from the consequences that could follow. Paul eventually realized that even though he had good intentions, it wasn't enough to change him or give him peace in his spirit. It is the same battle for Christians today. We attempt to live out our new life through old methods. However, the Lord God has given us the Holy Spirit. He is the power of God functioning as if Jesus was still here on earth. He has a role to make Jesus real to you. When you accept that truth, the Holy Spirit comes to live inside of your spirit and becomes one in your body for all eternity. Now you have a responsibility to live a Spirit-led life consistent with God's Word.

And His ministry does not stop there!

- He is the supernatural Helper that will cause you to remain in the position of rest and the position of peace that Jesus spoke about in the scriptures.
- He is the wisdom of God that causes you to express what is in God's mind and His heart.
- He is the Counselor that gives you the solution to issues outside of your natural capacity.
- The Holy Spirit is your Advocate.
- He causes you to pray in unlearned languages that are downloaded into your spirit and ultimately changes the atmosphere while simultaneously making confessions and declarations on your behalf.

- Through your heavenly language, you are warding off the attacks that the enemy has secretly plotted against you.
- The Holy Spirit is the Strengthener that will enable you to effectively live on this fallen earth and successfully prosper in all areas as you testify about Jesus.
- The Holy Spirit reveals the love of God and therefore enables you to receive all that He has done for you by grace.

Recall what Paul wrote to the Roman Church when he communicated how he tried to be a "good Christian." He had an impeccable résumé, which included a heap of knowledge stemming from the following:

- His parents were Pharisees who raised him under the strict guidelines of the law.
- He was born a Benjamite.
- He received extensive education on Jewish history.
- He was a lawyer.

The reason he highlights his credentials is that he wants believers to understand that no amount of education or generational influence can make you good enough. He said in the book of Philippians, chapter 3, that he counted all of those things as dung (human or animal waste), without Christ. Paul learned not to put his trust in his own knowledge. He expressed the frustration that is inevitable when a believer tries to teach himself how to live holy according to God's laws, as opposed to receiving grace through Christ and empowerment by the Holy Spirit (read John 14:26). If you want to experience all that God has intended for you, you will need to be filled with the power of the Holy Spirit with the evidence of speaking in tongues (read Acts 1:8 and Acts 2–4).

It is the same Holy Spirit power that causes Moses to split the Red Sea, Joshua to take down the walls of Jericho, Elisha to heal the Syrian of leprosy, Meshach, Shadrach, and Abednego to stand in the fiery furnace without getting burned, the power that performed miracles through Jesus, and even the power that resurrected Him from the dead. What a mighty God we serve.

In case you are wondering, neither Moses nor Joshua nor any of the prophets of old spoke in tongues. During that period, the Spirit of God did not live in human beings; He only hovered over them for a time. That hovering caused them to produce the results that only God can give. Fortunately, we are the chosen generation; the Lord has chosen to live inside of us. We are carriers of the anointing. The Lord does not hover over us for a moment and leave; He remains inside of us continually.

So, why wouldn't we open up our arms wide and receive all the free things that our Father has given us? He has blessed us with every spiritual blessing. It was His choice to equip us with spiritual weapons to defeat the devourer who awaits every opportunity to oppress God's children. In His wisdom, the Lord God hid His plan from Satan when He allowed His Son Jesus to be crucified. Why is that? It's because God uses instruments (people and things) that are less likely to be successful in accomplishing an assignment to shame those who believe they know it all and have it all. And that is what He has done with speaking in a heavenly language known as tongues.

The Bible says that when a believer speaks in tongues, he is not speaking to any human being, but he is speaking only with God. He does not even understand those spiritual words that he is speaking. However, by faith, we believe that we are releasing words that are making a transformational impact that is without boundaries in the spirit realm, manifesting itself in the physical realm in our favor.

A Christian filled with the Holy Ghost who practices speaking in tongues will have a radiance and strength about him that is unexplainable. Why? Because as you speak in tongues, the presence of God becomes overwhelmingly powerful over you. It ignites the fire! The Holy Spirit is the power that causes you to be even more zealous to tell others about Jesus and to do it effectively.

You will speak prophetic words, as the Holy Spirit will share things with you that otherwise you could not have seen.

I want to share a revelation with you that the Holy Spirit allowed me to see in the book of Luke, chapter 1. Earlier, I referenced the encounter that Zachariah had with the angel Gabriel. The messenger told Zachariah that his barren wife would become pregnant with his child and that the baby would be filled with the Holy Spirit inside of his mother's womb. That puzzled me, because according to the scriptures, it is only the Lord who can fill a person with His Spirit.

Elizabeth was not filled with the Holy Spirit, so how could the unborn child be filled? As I continued to ponder on this, the Holy Spirit opened my eyes! I want to share what He showed me. I will need to begin by recapping a visitation that Joseph, the husband of Mary, had. The angel of the Lord had appeared to Joseph and informed him that Mary (who was a virgin) would give birth to a Son who would be conceived by the Holy Spirit, who we know is Jesus Christ.

During Elizabeth's sixth month of pregnancy, she receives a visit from Mary, who is now pregnant with Jesus. Upon Mary's arrival, she greets Elizabeth, and the baby jumps inside of her womb, and immediately, Elizabeth is filled with the Holy Ghost. Wow! How many times have I read Matthew and Luke's account concerning this encounter, without recognizing the depth of what the Lord is showing us? Please bear with me as I explain further. I want you to see what I saw.

Do you remember the scripture in John, chapter 1, that says, in the beginning was the Word, and the Word was with God, and the Word was God? Well, in the fourteenth verse of that chapter, it also said that God manifested Himself and became flesh as the only begotten Son. All things considered, Mary, who was filled with the Spirit of God because of the fruit inside of her womb, spoke by the Spirit. I want to be clear in saying that Mary is not a deity. She was a mortal human being with human parents. God chose her for His purpose. In the same way, He has chosen you and me for His divine purpose. Let's continue.

When Mary spoke, filled with the Holy Ghost, Elizabeth received and was also filled. The scriptures continue by saying that Elizabeth spoke out in a loud voice. I have the scriptures posted below. Elizabeth, speaking through the Holy Spirit, is proclaiming that Mary is pregnant with the Lord. The Bible calls this prophesying. Soon after, Mary magnifies the Lord because she is feeling so favored that the Lord God chose her despite her status. You can read the entire prophecy in Luke 1:45–55.

Mary said to the angel, "How will this be since I am a virgin and have no intimacy with any man?" Then the

> angel replied to her, "The Holy Spirit will come upon you, and the power of the Most High will overshadow you [like a cloud]; for that reason, the holy (pure, sinless) Child shall be called the Son of God. And listen, even your relative Elizabeth has also conceived a son in her old age, and she who was called barren is now in her sixth month. (Luke 1:34–36 AMP)
>
> Now at this time Mary arose and hurried to the hill country, to a city of Judah (Judea), 40, and she entered the house of Zacharias and greeted Elizabeth. When Elizabeth heard Mary's greeting, her baby leaped in her womb; and Elizabeth was filled with the Holy Spirit and empowered by Him. And she exclaimed loudly, "Blessed [worthy to be praised] are you among women, and blessed is the fruit of your womb! And how has it happened to me, that the mother of my Lord would come to me? For behold, when the sound of your greeting reached my ears, the baby in my womb leaped for joy. And blessed [spiritually fortunate and favored by God] is she who believed and confidently trusted that there would be a fulfillment of the things that were spoken to her [by the angel sent] from the Lord." (Luke 39–45 AMP)

The Holy Spirit is genuinely our teacher. I have shared this revelation with you so you can appreciate and take advantage of everything that our Father has given to every one of us who believes Him. The Holy Spirit is not a feeling; He is a person. He wants to do things for you and through you. You can feel His presence, but that is not what validates His being. You can talk to Him, and you can trust that He hears you. When we embrace His ability with a teachable spirit, the Holy Spirit moves freely through our lives. Your relationship with the Lord will become so much sweeter. Can you have a relationship with the Lord without the infilling of the Holy Spirit? If you have received Jesus as your Lord, of course you can. But why not embrace everything He is willing to give? There is so much more God has for you.

Now, I would like to share this beautiful experience from 2012, only two months after my father passed on to be with the Lord. The significance of this testimony is that it helped me to embrace more of the Lord's supernatural love and grace.

SUPERNATURAL ENCOUNTER #3

A beautiful Saturday afternoon, I decided that I would join two of my boys, Blaine and my other son (by marriage), Travelle, for a run/walk on the track. I had been listening to music on my headset, and I felt the emotional pains of being distant from my father. In my spirit, I was conversing with the Lord, reverently, that I understood that my dad was enjoying the glorious heavens with Him. However, I was missing him so much. I remember thinking about how things must be so lovely for Daddy and that I should learn not to allow myself to react so selfishly.

My eyes and face flooded with tears of joy and sadness all at once. I didn't realize those types of emotions were even possible. Suddenly, my father's spiritual body, which looked like the young version of him I had never met, appeared next to me. He was jogging! I could not believe my eyes. He said, "Hey, my babe," in his sweetest accent. Then he zoomed ahead of me to position himself facing me; I had stopped jogging. He said, "Oh, Muttie (my nickname), it's beautiful (he was speaking of heaven)." Raising his hands to the air in excitement, he said, "Look at me ... no wheelchair!" Immediately, he flew up into the skies. He didn't have wings, but he flew! There was not an ounce of regret on his expression, only excitement.

Blaine was trailing closest on the track, so I ran over to him and described what had just happened in so much joy. Blaine was only eighteen years old. Most likely, he didn't know how to process all of this at once. It happened to me, and I was still trying to handle it. But I knew with no doubt that it was very real. My dad didn't have a care in the world. Words cannot describe his presence. I was extremely happy for him and even more grateful to my Lord Jesus!

I believe that the Lord allowed me to have that visitation with my father because I was sincerely looking into the heavens through the lens of His promises. I knew by faith that Daddy had joined the celebration in heaven. And the Lord allowed me to see a part of it through that encounter. The relevance of that testimony to the ministry of the Holy Spirit and speaking in tongues is that the Lord opens our minds to the realm of the supernatural, and the scriptures become alive in your spirit, revealing it to your mind. The process of transformation is taking place because your thoughts are being renewed to think God thoughts (his Word).

Speaking in tongues did not earn me that visitation. Graciously, the Lord in His love saw I was content in just believing him. Speaking in tongues did, however, draw me closer into the realm of the supernatural during my previous times of prayer, meditation, and worship. My tears were not tears of sorrow as though all was lost. They were tears of joy that Dad was with the Father and, simultaneously, tears of a human being missing the voice and physical presence of her earthly father, friend, and spiritual advisor whom she had, in later years, learned to appreciate.

I can easily recall, since a very early stage in my life, how afraid I was of dying. Once, as a child, I attended a funeral, and I noticed how the adults seemed to carry on as though they did not realize that one day their turn was coming. I asked my aunt, "How can everyone go about their business knowing they will soon get old and die?" She shrugged her shoulders with a grin and said, "I don't know; you just get used to it." Her answer frightened me even more. What was even more frightening was that none of us knew that spiritually we were all dead. Thankfully, today I know the truth, and I am no longer afraid. I have peace in my thoughts. We were spiritually removed from eternal darkness and placed into eternal light through Jesus Christ.

Believers, test our thoughts against God's Word. It is by faith we live out this life.

Review all of Hebrews, chapter 11, and see through the eyes of the patriarchs and the prophets as you relive their acts of faith. Abraham was a patriarch known as a friend of God. In faith, he believed God when He told him to move away from his relatives. How utterly courageous Abraham was to have acted on a voice he had never heard. This voice did not originate from anything earthly. No. The voice that spoke was from someone outside of the natural realm. The Alpha and Omega that caused his grandfather Noah to build the ark that saved his generation. The voice responsible for all things seen and unseen!

At seventy-five years old, the Lord told Abraham that he would make him a great nation, despite his wife, Sarah, being barren. He said that Abraham's seed would outnumber the countless stars. God wanted Abraham to see his remarkable ability, just as He had shown Noah how to build the ark through divine instructions. Think about it. God had Noah use specific materials so that the water would not seep into the boat. The Lord had considered the necessities to even stop the ship from tumbling. Isn't God amazing? This is His grace.

Because God has declared us righteous in Christ, we have everything we need to weather any storm. Our Father has placed a hedge of protection all around us, just as He set a hedge around Noah and his family. They didn't earn the right. Noah only trusted what God spoke. The Lord put Abraham to the test many times. His final evaluation was when he was ready and willing to sacrifice his son, whom he conceived miraculously with his barren wife, Sarah, the son God had promised him. Through faith, Abraham decided to carry it out. Through mercy, the Lord didn't take Abraham's son's life, but the Lord gave His own Son's life for the salvation of the world.

You did nothing to come into this world. It was God who chose to place you here. You cannot earn His love; He just does. He loves you so much that He would allow His Son to bear more suffering than anyone can imagine. Not only did Jesus endure the sufferings of physical pain, but even worse, He experienced the one thing that was most agonizing for Him; His Father, God Almighty forsook him. Meaning he was completely separated from God for that moment! What manner of love the Father has bestowed upon us that we should be called the sons of God?

The Lord has freely given us His Spirit to live inside of us because we believe His testimony about His Son. He didn't choose us with an agenda for us to fail but to succeed. So, He lives inside of us. Refuse to doubt and try to reason things out with your finite mind. Choose to embrace what the Father planned out for you before you even existed on this earth. Stand in His presence. Reflect on the gift He gave to those who were praying in the upper room in Acts, chapter 2. Ask Him to fill you up with His Holy Spirit power! Then, by faith, open your mouth and allow Him to speak through your vocal cords with no activity from your mind. If you believe, you will be filled!

Declare these declarations over yourself. Take a moment to meditate on your who you truly are. You are declared royalty in the household of God.

Your Father owns the universe!

He has chosen to give you authority, which is power to tread upon serpents and scorpions and over all the power of the enemy:

And nothing by any means shall hurt you.
Because you dwell in a place of power,
the place of advantage,
the place of dominion,
the place of authority,
the place of the anointing,
the place of divine health,
the place of wealth,
the place of love,
the place of peace.

And nothing and no one can snatch it from you because you are in the arms of the Most High! This is the love of the Father. Glory to Jesus! Are your eyes opening? Great!

Let's look at Adam.

CHAPTER 11

See His Love

We know that Adam was created in the (spiritual) image of God and that his physical body came from the dust of the earth, and God's breath gave him life. Adam was given dominion and authority over all of the earth, including every animal and creeping thing. He was given access to enjoy the wonderful things in the garden that God had grown for him—with one exception; he could eat from every tree except the tree of the knowledge of good and evil. Finally, God decided that Adam needed a companion. He caused Adam to fall asleep and basically performed surgery on him by removing a rib from his body, closing up his flesh, and creating another being that Adam called woman. He named her Eve.

Did Adam request any of these things? No. He couldn't have. So, what happened? Adam's Father chose to bless him with every good thing and gave him specific instructions to protect him. However, Adam chose to heed the voice of error as opposed to the voice of his Creator. He and his wife ate the forbidden fruit, releasing authority to the father of lies, the devil. Here is where we can take note of the first act of confusion. God is a God of order. Adam was warned that the day he disobeyed God by eating from that tree, he would surely die. And spiritually, he did.

Adam had been created from the dust. He had no mother, no baby stage, and no childhood. He was made a full-grown man with all that he needed. Think about that for a minute. He had an embedded knowledge of how to communicate and function on earth, much like a baby who instinctively knows how to suck, even in the womb. When God created Adam, He gave him all that was needed because of His nature, which is love, and His essence of perfection. Why was it so difficult for Adam to trust God completely by just believing what He said? Adam's disobedience caused him to be thrown out of the garden, which is out of God's presence, and now in darkness (ignorant of the truth).

You may even question, Why didn't God just forgive Adam and Eve and give them a second chance? Or why didn't God do a better job of stressing the consequences of Adam's betrayal? It is because God wanted Adam to trust every word He said as final. He wanted Adam to communicate through what is known as His revealed knowledge. And at God's time, he reveals more information, also known as higher truths, to you along the journey as you learn to trust Him more through obedience.

And furthermore, he did give Adam a second chance. It is through Jesus Christ. It was His mercy that sent them out of the garden instead of simply destroying mankind altogether. Had they remained in the garden, the possibility of their having access to the tree of life would have meant eternal corruption for man. Praise God forever more, who is wisdom Himself. Is your understanding of His love clearer?

Had Adam understood his identity as being the righteousness of God, he would not have acted in disobedience. Instead, he allowed himself to be adopted into the hands of the father of lies, the devil. How baffling. God did not want Adam to know pain, suffering, heartache, grief, death, or anything inconsistent with His nature. It was His love that caused him to shield Adam from these things. Adam's part was to believe Him. How could any child of God not believe that the Father's intentions are good? After all, it was of His own free will that He chose to bring you into this world.

Adam's disobedience, later described as sin, was the beginning of the fall of man. Jesus Christ, the second Adam, in His obedience is the rise of man, which is the resurrection, eternal life, and righteousness. Our Lord and Savior Jesus Christ brings us back into fellowship with God.

> The *great* patience of God was waiting in the days of Noah, during the building of the ark, in which a few, that is, eight persons [Noah's family], were brought

safely through the water. Corresponding to that [rescue through the flood], baptism [which is an expression of a believer's new life in Christ] now saves you, not by removing dirt from the body, but by an appeal to God for a good (clear) conscience, [demonstrating what you believe to be yours] through the resurrection of Jesus Christ. (1 Peter 3:20 AMP)

We are the chosen generation to show forth the praises of Jesus Christ through the power of the Holy Spirit. We are declared a royal priesthood, a holy nation. We are chosen to preach the Gospel of our Lord Jesus Christ to tell of the goodness and greatness of Jehovah God. We are to declare to all who will hear the love of the Father, who gave us the gift of salvation in Christ and has blessed us with every spiritual blessing that makes us who we are, a peculiar people. However, before we can do this, we must know of the Father's love personally.

And be renewed in the spirit of your mind. And that you put on the new man, which after God is created in righteousness and true holiness. (Ephesians 4:23 AMP)

The mind of Christ is righteousness and true holiness. (Ephesians 4:24 AMP)

Perhaps you're still unclear about what is righteousness and what is true holiness. Well, initially, I thought that my acts of kindness would make me righteous in God's eyes and that holiness was just impossible. As I reflect back to the year 2004, I was so excited about showing the Lord how much I could please him. I asked Him to send me to the places He needed me to go to do His work. I was so sure that the Lord was going to tell me to visit the sick in the nursing home or the hospitals and perhaps pray for them and maybe read Bible scriptures.

But instead, the Lord told me that my job was to teach my children

His Word and raise them in it. He told me that they were my priority to do His work. Wow! This was an eye-opener. "Okay, Lord," I said in shock. It just didn't seem as though I was really doing anything. These were my children. *I'm going to love them and expose them to your ways regardless. Shouldn't I focus on making an impact in other people's lives?* These were my honest thoughts. But in spite of them, I began reading scriptures more with my children.

Later in life, it came to my spirit what happened with Hannah and her son Samuel. God had answered Hannah's prayer of having a child. Because she was so grateful to the Lord, she freely gave him back to Him by allowing the man of God, Eli, to raise Samuel up in God's ways (His Word). She did this in appreciation toward the loving God that she served. Her trust in God was so great that she would give her two-year-old baby boy, whom she had desperately prayed for, over to a man of God to raise.

The Word of God is of that much importance. I finally received the revelation of why the Lord had given me those instructions. Jesus is the Word manifested in the flesh. Without God's Word, you cannot receive God. Another way to say that is, without Jesus, you cannot receive the Father (John 1:14, and the Word became flesh and dwelt among us). God was telling me to feed my children the true bread, the manna that came down from heaven. Just as Hannah was wise in understanding Samuel did not belong to her, I had to obtain that same type of God wisdom, that these children do not belong to me either.

If you read the story in 1 Samuel, chapter 1, Hannah keeps her baby boy to nurse him until he is able to grow into eating solid food, which is at two years old. She gives him over to the man of God so that he is able to mature the boy in God's ways. Every Christian is born a spiritual baby. We are taught the foundation of what salvation means. But eventually, just as Hannah recognized that her baby boy needed to mature, we too must recognize the necessity for growth in our spiritual maturity. To have the mind of Christ is to know who you are in Christ. Jesus is righteousness. We obtain our righteousness through everything that He settled for us at the cross. It is not our works that make us righteous but rather our belief that we are righteous in Jesus.

Because Hannah believed God had given her a son, she willingly gave him back to whom he rightfully belonged. Samuel, the prophet, was raised up according to God's character, God's Word. God blessed me with three precious children from my womb. And I love them dearly. But I thank God that I finally realized that I could never love them as much as God loves them. My job was to not only nurse them but also to feed them what the man of God fed Samuel, God's Word.

We have the mind of Christ. Whether or not we choose to water our gardens with the Word of God is up to us. God wants us to come up hither (to a higher level of knowing Him). As a babe, your vision of the Father is somewhat like a fairy tale. You believe that God is so far off into the skies. Most likely, you don't feel as though you are in God's thoughts. You take into consideration all of the people in this world. There is no way the Lord has time for you, so you take a chance and suspiciously ask Him to help you. It seems like sometimes He says yes, but other times He either says no, or He just doesn't pay attention to your request at all. He has His hands full. This sounds so silly today because of the relationship that I now have with the Father. I painted Him as a deadbeat dad. I was oh so wrong!

During my late twenties, the Lord probed my thoughts. These were some of the questions: What does it mean to be God? Does He want me to need Him, or should I be smart enough to make the right choices? My parents didn't choose me, and I didn't choose them. Does that mean God chose them for me, and me for them?

These are the types of questions that used to visit my thoughts. It's because of human beings' instinctive nature of wanting to be loved, accepted, chosen, and feel exceptionally favored. The Lord was probing me with such questions because He wanted me to consider His greatness even more than what I thought I knew.

A born-again Christian's life in the physical world has issues that are still in place from before he/she received salvation. The Lord is aware of this. Then what do we do? The answer is quite simple; you were never meant to do it on your own strength or with your kind of knowledge. God has given us His Word and the Holy Spirit as our Helper. He is the powerful agent that causes you to function beyond your limited capacity. Your understanding is heightened, and your words are spoken from the inward man.

We were intentionally created with emotions so that we could share in His great love! No one on this earth wants to feel unloved. A baby who is right out of his mother's womb longs for the same undeserved security. It's that feeling of protection that circumferences him/her on every side. As we mature, we continue to hold on to that inner desire of wanting to be loved, nurtured, and protected. It is purposely embedded inside of us.

God created the universe. Please stop reading for a minute and close your eyes to think about what that means. Did you think about the things that consist within it? The heavens and above, the earth and below, the sun the moon and the stars. What if one day the sun didn't come up, and the moon and stars suddenly disappeared? How would you call them back? Can you call them back? What if the skies suddenly opened up and all you could see was a void?

What if the rain no longer came down? The only available water would be the existing waters in the oceans, the rivers, and the seas, which would eventually dry up. What would you do? What could you do? Who would you call? Would science give an explanation as to why water has become suddenly extinct? Or why the sun and the moon will no longer bring forth their light? How can anyone begin to comprehend the dramatic downfall of what we know as natural events? Man would only be at the mercy of God. But what if you don't know Him? You would inevitably blame Him for not giving you something that you didn't even earn, nonetheless deserve, in the first place. He chose to freely give it to you out of the abundance of His grace.

Remember what happened to Jonah? God gave him a message to give to the children on Nineveh that he didn't want to give. The message was that God was going to destroy all of them because of their evil ways. Jonah grew angry because God showed mercy on the Ninevites and didn't harm them. In his anger, he decided that he wanted to die.

He sat in the scorching sun waiting to die, until God grew a tree over him to give him shade. He was so comfortable with the shade he decided he wanted to live. In His wisdom, God caused the cankerworm to eat up the tree, preventing Jonah from enjoying the royalties of that shade that he didn't even deserve. He had not grown the tree. It was only God who chose to bless him with shade.

God has chosen us out of His great love for us.

As you mature in the truth, you no longer think like a child. Now, you have the mind of Christ.

- You have come to the understanding that the same Father that Jesus spoke to as He walked on this earth is also your Father.
- Your understanding is enlightened that God has chosen you, and you didn't choose Him, and therefore He expects and desires for you to call upon Him.
- You have fellowship with your Father and hear Him speak answers to your spirit, and He gives you direction because you expect to receive His guidance.
- You no longer see the Father as a supernatural being so far away, but you see the supernatural, mighty God inside of you.
- You lean into Him, and He causes you to feel closer than ever to Him.
- You believe that the answer came, and He is seated at the right hand of the Father, and you are in Him. Therefore, you are at rest.
- You understand that Jesus meant it when He said it is finished.
- You think soberly because you possess the inspiration of the scripture, and it has been deposited in your spirit.
- You are at another level. You are aware that you are not of this world. You are from above. Your Father has chosen you to tell the world of His goodness.
- He has called you as a vessel to pour out the thoughts that He has put in your heart.
- You now have His very nature because you know who you are and whose you are.
- You no longer lust after the things of the world.
- You are not conformed to the evil, wicked ways you once possessed, but you are being transformed every day, more and more like Jesus!
- There is a new fire inside of you to tell about the goodness of the Lord Jesus and all that He has done for you.
- You know that your adversary is the devil, and he would love for you to fall into the same old trick he used on Adam. But praise

God that you have the mind of Christ, and the Holy Spirit reveals his plans to you ahead of time.

It was never about a piece of fruit. Just like it's never about whatever challenge you find yourself in. It is always about knowing what God has said, believing it, and living it no matter what. Glory to Jesus! Congratulations! You are progressing. Let's continue and look into the thoughts that cause so many of us to question what God wants to do in our lives.

Many of us find ourselves afraid to disappoint God. As mentioned earlier, regarding patriarchs and prophets, we look at our present capabilities and begin to create visions of failure that actually paralyze our actions. The Bible says that faith without works is dead. The very meaning of death is lifelessness. So, to act in faith is on the living word. Jesus said that He set before us life and death, but He wishes that we choose life. This can only mean that not acting in faith means we are afraid to live.

If we consider that faith comes by hearing the Word of God, then we can begin to see the relevance of studying and understanding God's Word. Jesus said that His purpose for coming was to give us an abundant life. He has given life to every believer through confession of His resurrection. Now he wants us to live in that abundance by trusting in all that He has said concerning this new life. He performed many signs and wonders by the power of the Holy Ghost. We have that same ability, because we also possess the indwelling presence of the Holy Spirit. He said that signs and wonders shall follow the believers.

That statement alone brings a great amount of expectation of a believer. What if it doesn't work? It's no different from questioning your very salvation. This is why we must renew our minds to think like our Creator so that we may see as He sees. So that we may envision truths and know them to be final according to His Word and refuse to give attention to the lies of the enemy.

I recall the encounter I shared with you earlier as my spirit separated from my body. Looking back on that glorious day with knowledge, I thank God for revealing Himself to me. He showed me His power and His ownership of me.

God's Word unveils His loving, caring, merciful goodness. My mind is being renewed day by day to think more and more like Jesus. I am not afraid to trust God and know that what He says is true. He said that I am alive in Christ and that I will be with Him forevermore; so, it's true.

Confidence in God is confidence in His Word, which is acting out in faith, which is living!

Choose life by meditating on God's Word. Choose life by looking unto Jesus in the midst of any circumstance. Visualize the good things in life that He has placed in your heart. Speak those things into being by praying and making declarations and confessions, saying what God's Word says about them.

Today's technology has made it so much more resourceful for us as believers. Any area that you need to pray about, you can Google for scriptures surrounding that topic. Watch as a fire ignites from inside while you meditate and study. Align your actions with those words by being conscious of what you have read throughout your day.

In the Bible days, when God spoke through His prophets, the king had two options—to heed God's Word or choose to ignore and trust in his own ability. King David committed an evil deed when he slept with Uriah's wife and caused her to become pregnant. Uriah was a soldier in David's army. King David sent out orders for the young man to report to him. David deceitfully plotted to have Uriah go to Bathsheba, his wife, and lay with her in an effort to cover his sin.

The humble soldier refused to be with his wife while his brethren were out fighting in the war. He chose to sleep at his doorstep, where everyone could openly see his decision not to lay with his wife. David in his selfish and murderous act had Uriah killed. Later, the prophet Nathan revealed to David how God had seen his act and was quite displeased with him. David heeded the voice of God, repented, fasted, and prayed.

The significance in this is that David knew that the prophet spoke God's Word, and he also knew that he needed to act with a repentant heart. Although David sinned, as he was reprimanded, he behaved as though he was chastised as a child by his father. And with that mind-set, he is described as a man after God's own heart. God wants us to know Him by knowing His ways, which is His Word.

There is something that God has put in your spirit. You get excited when you think about it. It seems to come very naturally to you. But for some reason, you tend to feel challenged about taking that dream and making it a reality. You seem to think, *This thing that I do so well is good, but I can't take it seriously.* Why not? Of course, you can. You've just got to make sure you channel it right. There are many talented people in this world who are very successful. Many of them don't even know Jesus Christ as their personal Lord and Savior. But they have talent that has been purposed for greatness.

However, they must come into the kingdom of light so that darkness does not overshadow those things that God originally intended for good. Darkness brings about a selfish, egotistical mentality. It births greed, envy, cruelty, and a desire for things that are wicked. Although initially it is not as obvious, in time, the manifested fruits such as depression, suicide, anger, bitterness, loneliness, and so much more eventually surface.

Consider Moses. He was predestined to become the chosen one to lead the Israelites out of Egypt. Even though the order was given to kill every male child born of a Hebrew woman, those orders could not apply to God's chosen vessel to lead his children out of Egypt. Moses's life was spared, and he was raised as a son unto Pharaoh. He was taught their ways. However, the hand of God was upon Moses, and this is what caused Moses to now thirst after righteousness. He found himself questioning the things that were happening around him, and he later discovered his true identity.

Why was I spared? He looked upon the affliction of his people, and he realized these were his brothers, and he shared their fate. All the while, he had been behaving as an enemy to his mother and father. How many lashings, cruelty, and deaths did they suffer as he slept comfortably in the palace?

Moses had an unexplainable knowing that there had to be something more that he could not see just yet. But what? He attempted to come to the rescue of a Hebrew slave by murdering one of the pharaoh's men. And he also tried to influence a leadership of peace among the brethren as he discouraged a fight between two Hebrew brothers. But instead, he was attacked by being reminded of his decision to murder the Egyptian guard.

As we learn later, Moses flees into the desert and later meets his wife,

Zipporah, and lives there for forty years. During his stay, he is introduced to the true God of the Hebrews. Moses quickly transitions from being a son in the house of Pharaoh to a shepherd who later comes to know of the God I Am! It is at the burning bush that God performs signs and wonders right before the eyes of Moses. The beauty of reading this is that God was as instrumental then as He still is today, that everything He did was done strategically perfectly.

God told Moses that He would make him a god over Pharaoh. Imagine that. God put fear inside of Pharaoh as Moses came before him. This is mind-blowing. Anywhere that we go in this world, when we go in the power of God, He causes us to rule over a situation. He causes our words to have an anointing that commands authority. The Bible says that we have been declared kings and priest unto God. Why? For His divine purposes. It is never about the circumstance but the results of God's purpose to come to pass.

Training is through trials and tribulations. A parent teaches his/her child how to respond. There are times when the child knows what to do and how to handle a situation because of proper training, but there are also times when the child must report to the parent and follow the instructions given on how to handle a matter. In some cases, after giving the report to the parent, the child just waits confidently, knowing that their Father is handling the matter.

Prophets of God had already spoken concerning the bondage that the Israelites would suffer and that a deliverer would come to free them. This is a shadow of what was to come with the Savior of not only the Hebrew tribe but the entire world. The bondage was not only about the physical but more so the spiritual affecting the physical. The mother of Moses secured her baby in a basket and placed him in a river with crocodiles and other ferocious creatures of the water, trusting in the God of Abraham, Isaac, and Jacob.

She sent her young daughter Miriam to follow and to find out where God would lead him. Moses flowed with the anointing of the Spirit of God that shut the mouths of the crocodiles, caused the rivers to flow smoothly, and caused the wind to guide him. This baby boy had no control over the direction of the flow of his vehicle; it was all led by God! Glory!

> And we know, that all things work together for good to them that love God, for those that are called according to His purpose. (Romans 8:28 AMP)

How troubling this must have been for Yoshabel. Where did the idea come from? What sense did it make? What did she subject her baby boy to? A slow death? The only conclusion is that she trusted God. A believer lives a life that is peculiar. You do things the natural man cannot comprehend. You may even look back on occasion and question why you are so drawn to do something you are not confident about but feel so strongly within. As you are reminded who you are, you continue in your faith and allow the power of God to work out all the details of whatever that thing is He has drawn you to do. The Bible has given instruction to trust in the Lord with all your heart, and He will direct your path.

Moses could not have had a smooth canoe ride, no more than many of the challenges we undergo as believers. The alligators and crocs in the water can easily represent those who speak against you in front of you and behind your back. The wretched things that you come to learn have been said about you can cause you to question if you have what it takes to continue on. The wavy, violent waters can represent the financial challenges that try to drown you in so much sorrow and shame. Discouraging thoughts tend to build up against you no matter how many confessions you make over yourself. The winds become fierce as more and more problems arise concerning relationships within your very home.

But thanks be to God who always causes us to triumph in Christ Jesus! He causes us to fall on our knees and cry out His name, knowing that He alone is God. Don't be ruled by emotions. Jesus himself cried out to the Father in the Garden of Gethsemane right before his crucifixion. His request to God was, *If there be any other way, let this cup pass from me, but nevertheless, let Your will be done.*

We have the mind of Christ. Yoshabel didn't think like an Egyptian. She was Hebrew. She had higher standards for herself because she served the Most High God. Even though she wore rags stained in mud mixture, and most likely even blood accumulated from the many wounds of the harsh working conditions and the taskmaster's whips, Yoshabel knew she was favored over those who did not know God.

Don't just dwell on the earth; dwell in Him while on earth. To live life with this mentality is to truly trust God, knowing how much He loves you. This information is supplanted into those who dwell in the secret chambers of the Most High. Expressions and verbal language are insufficient to express the love, perfection, protection, comfort, and peace that are unleashed by the Giver of life. So indulge in Him. He will open your inside to see His heart. He will cause you to dig deep into the springs of His anointing as you pray, worship, study, study scriptures, and fast—not because you feel obligated to but because you desire to drink.

FINAL WORD

The entire Word of God is all about Jesus! He is the spoken Word of God and the focal point of everything, as God has made Him so. Don't be afraid; be free. This is the most liberating reality you will ever dare to experience. You can do all things but only through Christ who strengthens you because you believe Him.

Once you realize this, the grinding chains of confusion, depression, anxiety, loneliness, obsessions, deprivation, abandonment, false worshipping of issues and emotions that you've made god over your decisions, addictions, pride, envy, low self-esteem, inappropriate language and behaviors, hostile attitudes, sexual immoralities, the inability to give and receive love, nervous breakdowns, psychotic behaviors, feelings of emptiness, bitterness, and any other form of darkness that has tried to halt your destiny—they are all placed under the subjection of the authority of the powerful name of Jesus.

He took each of them and all other forms of darkness upon His flesh for you, me, and everyone else in this world. Each was spiritually deposited on His sin-free body. Each lashing that He suffered was for your healing. The emptiness and abandoned state that He experienced from Jehovah God, His Father, was all so that you would never be forsaken. Everything that He did was out of love and obedience to the Lord God. It wasn't easy for Jesus, and it wasn't easy for God the Father.

The spiritual battle that took place at Calvary was for our freedom from the prison of eternal damnation.

My daddy left a seed on earth, without even realizing he had planted it. It was the seed of a little girl gazing at her father feeling broken but looking up to the Lord with hope. That imagery remains strong in my spirit, not out of pity but out of a grateful heart. Today, my father is gazing in the eyes of Master with tears of joy, while I continue to embrace His love by sharing the truth with others. You are chosen! We are so blessed. It is finished!

Prayer of Feeling Grateful

My Father who is in heaven.

My Father who has given me salvation in my Lord Jesus.

My Father who has placed His Spirit inside of me.

Thank You for Your love.

Thank You for Your grace.

Thank You for Your wisdom.

Thank You for Your counsel.

Thank You for Your strength.

Thank You for Your power.

Thank You for peace.

Thank You for choosing me as Your child.

I am forever grateful for the supernatural exchange that has taken place for me.

You took my old sinful nature and pinned it on Jesus.

And You gave me a new nature that is everything good that came out from Jesus.

I reject ignorance, and I embrace truth that is only found in Your Word.

The truth that I am righteous in Christ.

The truth that says I am born again.

The truth that says You laid out a plan for my life even before my mother pushed me out of her belly.

The truth that says You have made provisions for me to succeed.

The truth that says no trap the enemy tries to set against me will work any longer.

You show me the good path.

You train me how to stay on the course to progression.

You honor me with the comfort of Your presence during the times of strengthening.

You fight the battles I was never meant to fight.

You remind me to look only at Jesus, especially when I am tempted to do it my way.

You are the greatest gift.

Your love is incomprehensible and unexplainable.

Forever I am grateful.

In Jesus's name. Amen.

Prayer for Encouragement

My Father in heaven whom I trust with every fiber of my being.

I kneel before Your altar in the spirit and in the truth of Your Word.

Thank You for advancing my steps every day to know more and more of who You are and who I am according to Your Word.

I give You the weight of my worries. I place them in the hands of my Lord Jesus Christ.

In exchange, I take into my being Your strength, Your might, Your wisdom, Your peace, and Your grace.

In faith, I choose to trust the plans that You have for me.

In faith, I choose to believe that the expected end works for my good.

In faith, I close my eyes to frustration, and I open my eyes to the wisdom of Your divine will.

Your Word tells me to be patient and pray without trying to figure things out on my own, so I will.

Your Word says that as I wait patiently in prayer. You give me the grace to press on in spite of those issues.

Your Word tells me to praise You with my lips, with my spirit in the midst of the pressures.

You have said in Your Word that in my brokenness You increase Your Holy Spirit power of grace working in me.

Because You have said it, it is final. I believe You.

I choose to trust You as David trusted You when he was running for his life.

I choose to trust You as the three Hebrews trusted You and allowed themselves to be placed in the fire.

I choose to trust You as Jesus trusted that You would raise Him back to life after He allowed Himself to be put to death.

I choose You, Lord.

I choose You, the Life Giver.
I choose You, the King of kings.
I choose You, the Master.
I choose You who are Wisdom.
I choose You who are the Prince of Peace.
I choose You who are the Great I Am.
I choose You who reminds me of my position of righteousness.
I choose the author of every seen and unseen thing.
I surrender my understanding and count it as foolish.
I follow You, Lord.
Open my eyes and teach me to see through Your lens.
I am willing. So have Your way.
In Jesus's name. Amen.

Prayer to Receive Salvation

God of the universe who is over all that I see and don't see, I confess to You that I am a sinner. I am choosing to receive the gift of salvation by acknowledging that I was born into a world of corruption. So, You sent Jesus the Messiah to wash me with His blood and give me a new life of incorruption. Forgive me of my sins. I believe that Jesus sacrificed Himself for me, and I declare that He is Lord over my life. I give Jesus all of my hurt, and I take all of His peace and His joy. I am born again. The old corrupted nature that I was once born into is buried now with those fruits of failure, disgrace, lust, and any other form of bondage. I am a new creation who is born of the Spirit of the living God!

Prayer of Reflection

Lord Jesus,

Never in my years on this earth could I have ever imagined such love as what You have poured over me. Despite my failures, You have blessed me with a supernatural affection that the natural realm cannot relate to. What is this type of love that is so forgiving, faithful, and gentle to the undeserving? I can only say that I will serve You all the days of my life. I choose to surrender my thoughts, my desires, my will, my entire being all to You.

I am Your servant now and forever more because You have made Your love known to me, even in my inward parts, beyond my heart's affection and emotions. Continue to wash me daily with Your Word. I welcome the opportunity to bathe in the purity of Your flesh. Clean me through and through with the living Word that purges any unclean thing from my thoughts.

I surrender, Lord. Have Your perfect way. I trust You, Lord. I trust You, my God. Thank You for Your grace. Thank You for Your peace. Thank You for Your love.

Prayer of Praise to God's Awesomeness

Almighty God, You are infinite in all Your ways. (God's ways are higher than man's.)

You created heaven and earth.

My limited intelligence could only see fleshy imaginations.

From the dust, You formed me and gave me life beyond comprehension. (God is the giver of life.)

In a fallen state, I was covered in shame, until You gave me Truth, and now I reign. (Jesus is Truth.)

You cradled me with Your wings of protection.

Even in my ignorance, You chose to never leave me or forsake me (God's promise to the believer).

You are the one true God, who I magnify from within my spirit.

Oh, praise the name of Jesus!

Thank You, Lord, that You knew my ways and thoughts were futile.

You sent Your Word ahead of me, and in mercy, You made a way. (Before time was, Jesus existed as the Word.)

You are Wisdom Himself who has redeemed me by Your Word.

You are Righteousness Himself who has made me righteous by Your Word.

You are the Most High God who has made me Your living tabernacle. (The Holy Spirit lives in a believer.)

And now I live connected to the true vine, eternally grateful, eternally at rest, all by Your grace.

Prayer of Worship and Declarations

Lord, You are the author and the Finisher of my Faith.

I worship You from my spirit with my soul and my body.

I offer praises and thanksgiving that goes up before Your alter as incense.

Thank you for your presence, Your might, your counsel, and your wisdom.

Thank you for giving me the privilege to appear before your throne of grace where mercy abounds for me.

As I bow my knees in prayer, I am strengthened in the inner man knowing that I am bowing before power; the Creator who is invisible, but whom I know (through your Word).

I believe your testimony, which is now my testimony, that declares Jesus Christ as Lord and Savior over me.

You have given me the witness of the Holy Ghost in my spirit to see Jesus Christ crucified and resurrected in His righteousness for me.

He is alive, and He is seated at your right hand, and you have placed me inside of Him assuming that same position of authority and righteousness in His name.

Therefore, I am above principalities, spiritual wickedness, and every other form of darkness.

Through my prayers, I am spiritually elevated to see clear.

From the heavens, you disperse your ministering angels on my behalf.

You have made me your child; I am divinely connected to you. You have given me your spirit of boldness, your word of Truth.

So, who is man whose breath is in his nostrils that I should be afraid to speak or go anywhere, or afraid to expect supernatural results that are only produced by You Most High?

Your word says every detail in my life is well

My health, my thoughts, my mind, my family, my finance, and any assignment you give me.

Because your desire is for me to prosper and have a long life.

What manner of love is this that I should be called your child? I am grateful to call you, Father.

You have made me a member of the household of faith.

In your divine wisdom, you have made Jesus, my Master; and as His servant, I am entirely yielded to serve Him with all of me. I am a slave to Christ.

Through the Holy Ghost power that is at work in me, I am stepping out every day in faith; walking the path of the just.

Even when I am physically still, I am on the move in my spirit. Things in the natural are lining up for me. I have a goodly heritage.

Any word that is spoken against me, they do not bring fruit because I am sealed in the power of your dwelling tent. I am barricaded in your anointing so those evil words can only trickle down.

You have shown me the way. So I walk in that truth. I walk in that authority. I call things that be not as though they were. So any plot of the enemy to strategize against my progress, I cancel and nullify those plans. I cover my family and me in the blood of Jesus. The blood of Jesus speaks of better things.

I declare that my future is set and secured. I trust in your word that is a lamp unto my feet and a light unto my path.

I shall continue to give you praises in spite of challenges my Father because I trust you. My praises to you are not in ignorance but in the knowledge of who you are. I

I am excited in my spirit, Lord, because I know the devil is a liar. I am excited in my spirit, Lord, because I know your word is truth. I am excited because I am a winner.

I am a woman/man of influence who receives answers.

You make my words impactful. Any concerns in my life are temporary, and you give me the wisdom to respond accordingly.

You cause me to discern rightly, so I do not walk in error, and I do not receive error. Therefore, any wicked thoughts that come to me even as I pray, you alert me in the inner man.

I do not give attention to the lies of the enemy, but I choose to hear from you.

I lie at your feet at the place of rest in peace; under your wings of protection,

Yay though I walk through the valley of the shadow, that may sometimes cause me to question a situation, I thank you that you bring your word to my memory and the truth prevails out of my lips.

You have not made me ignorant to the devices of the enemy; you have given me the mind of Christ; I receive counsel from the supernatural, which manifests in my life and my family's life.

Thank you for your love; I love you because you first loved me. You have taught me love. You have given me love. You have demonstratedand continue to express true love.

To You be all the glory! In Jesus name. Amen.

Devotional 1

> And I was with you in weakness, and in fear and in much trembling. And my speech and my preaching was not with enticing words of man's wisdom, but in demonstration of the Spirit and of power. That your faith should not stand in the wisdom of men, but in the power of God. (1 Corinthians 2:3–5 KJV)

God created human beings just because He wanted to. Since His character is just, we can only conclude that He had good thoughts in mind when He created us. So, why would we ever question His motives? Why don't we inventory our own motives and then measure them against God's Word?

God is God alone. He does not share His glory with man. He takes all the glory, and we willingly give it to him by yielding to His Word. But how do we yield continually? We do it by recognizing that the power of God is ultimate in everything. The Lord resists the proud, but He opens up more favor and opportunities to the humble. Resist the urge to reason as an ordinary man/woman and choose to listen to the counsel of the Holy Spirit.

Paul wanted the Corinthian church to recognize his personal weaknesses and fears, so that they could adjust their lens to see the power of God at work in him in spite of his challenges. It's easy to contact an attorney to begin divorce proceedings. It's easy to quit your job on the spot because your supervisor has disrespected you and does not recognize your value. It's easy to blow up on your spouse, sibling, colleague, or the stranger at the grocery store who grabbed the last item you were just about to grab. It's easy to blow off steam and say derogatory things. But each of these actions has negative consequences. They give room to the enemy.

However, when you wait patiently upon the Lord because you choose to trust Him, He releases His supernatural wisdom and His power-packed anointing that charges you up and gives you a confidence that cannot be explained. The Lord will begin to download heavenly channels of communication that translate you to higher levels. The issues that initially dominated your thoughts will become meaningless. The Lord will reveal intricate details. That is the power of God at work in a human being.

So, take charge by allowing the Maker to be in charge. Refuse to look at man's ability and give God the glory by being a yielded vessel. Allow Him to do what only He can. Be conscious of everything that our Lord Jesus has paid for. God bless you.

Devotional 2

> Now when Daniel knew that the writing was signed, he went into his house; and his windows being open in his chamber toward Jerusalem, he kneeled upon his knees three times a day, and prayed, and gave thanks before his God, as he did aforetime. (Daniel 6:10–11 KJV)

Daniel was known as having an excellent spirit. He, along with his other Hebrew brothers and sisters, had been forced into slavery. Darius, who was acting king, grew to love Daniel. However, this relationship sparked jealousy among the king's entourage. Two of Darius's men plotted against him by tricking the king into endorsing what could have been Daniel's execution. Despite the plans against him, Daniel gave God thanks and submissively continued in prayer as he had done before.

Jesus Christ has made us righteous in the sight of the Lord our God. The consciousness of that truth keeps us focused on His promises. The scripture highlights that Daniel looked out of an open window and fixed his eyes on Jerusalem, and then he began to pray. I am almost certain that Daniel's prayers were emotionally burdensome for the fate of his people. But in spite of the turmoil going on in his thoughts, his mind was made up to trust that God was his vindicator. The order was given to throw Daniel in the lion's den. But the Lord changed the appetites of the lions, and they could not devour him.

This earth is fallen, and those birthed forth from it remain in spiritual bondage to this day. God has chosen to redeem those who sincerely call upon the name of Jesus. Why? Because He has decided to rescue and graciously give life to all who believe He can save them.

Although a Christian is saved and will not suffer eternal separation from God, we are still in this world with its accessories of bitterness, jealousy, hate, division, and all the lustful things inclusive. Our position is to remain in the same posture as demonstrated in the Bible verse. Refuse to give attention to the lies of the enemy that are futile to your destiny. Choose to withstand the pressures of life in the power of His might.

Television commercials can cause you to question your health because the advertisement agencies have strategized to boost their sales at your expense. Deceptively, they encourage you to get checked for this and that and so forth. The goal is to stimulate fear in your thoughts, which will eventually lead you to act according to their assumptions. It's wise to receive yearly checkups, but it's foolish to not recognize when an entity wants to control you.

Stay focused! Spend time in the Lord's presence through daily prayer, worship, and meditations on His Word. The satraps recognized Daniel's prayer time as a weakness that worked against him. Unfortunately for them, prayer was and still is the dominant force that activates change and produces the results of what God's Word says (James 5:16)!

"As many as are led by the Spirit of God, they are the sons of God" (Romans 8:14).

Fix your eyes on the Lord Jesus, and He will exonerate you!

God bless you.

Afterword

How the book came into being…

As a child, I was curious about the higher power that "possibly existed. I did not realize that the direction that I had taken to finally have a personal relationship with the Lord, took much longer than it needed to. My ignorance became the driving force of wanting to share the love of God with others.

Four years ago, The Holy Spirit told me to write this book. He said, "Let them know that I love them despite their failures." He showed me my frustrations through ignorance, then He revealed to me His peace that I now enjoy through the true knowledge of Him.

I pray that this book ignites a desire in its readers to step outside of the natural and look for the supernatural through God's word, and not manmade imaginations. This book represents my personal walk with the Lord. It is meant to encourage others to either begin their own relationship with Him or develop and press for an even greater one.

The Lord reveals more and more of His nature to His children INDIVIDUALLY through His word…. taste and see that the Lord is good. Surely, you will witness His greatness in your life. God bless you.

Printed in the United States
By Bookmasters